Color in Flower Arrangement

COLOR in

Arrangement

ADELAIDE B. WILSON

COLOR PHOTOGRAPHY BY ROCHE

Flower

M. BARROWS AND COMPANY, INC.

PUBLISHERS, NEW YORK

My World of Color   8

1 Color: As We Know It

2 Color: As We Use It

CONTENTS

3 Color: Where We Find It

ILLUSTRATIONS
in color
following page 104

MY WORLD OF COLOR

Only recently has flower arrangement begun to take its proper place as a decorative art in the western world. Before you challenge this assertion of its high place, look back over the history of art.

Plant forms have been an inspiration to artists for thousands of years. The lotus of Egypt, the acanthus of Greece, the rose of Persia have been exquisitely used in the architecture and ornament of many peoples. Grapes and pomegranates, olives and lilies are the cherished symbols of religious art. In medieval tapestries, flowers were worked in such flawless detail that they have become botanical records. Fruits and flowers cover the ceramics of the great French and German and English potters. In China and Japan, flower arrangement has been taught for centuries as an important artistic pursuit, and every lovely screen, vase, and silken robe is adorned with chrysanthemum, lotus bud, or branch of pine. Is all this not evidence that arrangements of flowers have long been an accepted form of artistic expression?

The student today may well take time to analyze the qualities which give beauty to the old designs. In flower painting of the Flemish and Dutch masters of the sixteenth and seventeenth centuries are many lessons. Adaptations of these arrangements with fresh flowers seldom suit our streamlined life today; nor is there often time to evolve such opulent pieces. But they teach us that in natural beauty—in flower, bud, butterfly, bird, and rock, there is rich inspiration.

Few humans are indifferent to a spectacle in Nature. Tastes may differ in books read, plays seen, music heard, and clothes worn. We question the good taste of those whose choices differ from ours. Yet a hillside of flowering dogwood, a mountain sunset, or a storm at sea calls forth unanimous murmurs of appreciation. I have seen a homeward-bound crowd in Manhattan, weary and impatient because of an inconvenient thunderstorm, suddenly lose its tensions and pause congenially to watch a rainbow arch over the skyscrapers.

There are less spectacular beauties, too. A butterfly which appears a white flutter near a flower, on closer inspection reveals topaz and sapphire markings of intricate design. Often when the petals have fallen from a flower, the pollen-shorn stamens rise from a calyx fully as exquisite as the blossom it held. The sepals of a flower provide a surprisingly different color scheme which went unnoticed in a superficial glance at what appeared to be a dead blossom. Perhaps you, too, have been puzzled by a strange-appearing bird which is really the scarlet tanager in his moulting season coat of many colors. These few examples show how limitless is our source for study of color, and how available.

The contemporary flower arranger sees in her materials something beyond just an ornament for her home or a wedding or a shop window. The bounty of Nature offers constant challenge to create something which is in its essence a work of art.

Museums have opened their doors to the flower arranger and invited her to display her work with their more permanent treasures.

While a flower arrangement is necessarily an ephemeral form of expression, memory recalls and photographs record many truly-fine pieces of floral art. No longer are plants and blossoms simply a basis for another art form, but, well designed, they present an art form of their own.

While flower arrangement has been developing so richly, its practitioners have had little important literature to guide them. They have studied design as it has been applied to painting or sculpture, and for information on color, they have wandered through the devious paths of industrial art and color psychology, finding only here and there useful nuggets, and these not related to color in living substances.

Long before I ventured into arranging, I had been collecting facts about color. It is a subject of enormous fascination. I hoarded morsels from experience, by hearsay and from reading, with the lack of discrimination of a small boy who crams his pockets with varied and remarkable loot. There followed a more sedate pursuit through formal study and applied art. While I still cannot comprehend some of the scientific disputes on color, I respect these peaks of learning as a Boy Scout venerates the conquest of Mt. Everest.

Out of such a welter of color miscellany this book has grown. My mental pockets have been turned inside out and the contents carefully sorted to share the facts which I think will be most useful to you as a flower arranger. This discussion of color as we know it, use it, and find it is the result of years of actual experience as an arranger and a judge. My study has often resulted from a search for answers to the questions which have come to me as I lectured and taught. Some of the observations have grown from my own necessity to solve problems which my own mistakes have posed.

At times I have contracted uncomfortable skin poisonings from creeping over rocks or under shrubs for a closer scrutiny of a colorful lichen or a gay insect. For this I have endured the scorn of friends who insist that if I must pry into the intimate life of plants and insects, I deserve all I get. The superficial irritation leaves me long before the memory of a magic color harmony fades. I shall continue to pry, and hope you will follow suit.

Beyond an introduction to color as it concerns flower arrangers, this book has a further purpose. I trust it proves that any subject which has as many facets as color—the lifework of men for centuries and still a challenge to the best minds today— must be subject to a wide range of interpretation. Certainly color should never be used as a brake to creativeness but rather as a spur to imagination and a key which opens a door to a more seeing view of the rich, living forms of Nature.

Only with the help of faithful friends could I ever have tailored my colorful fragments to fit inside book covers. While all this has been written without notes, and from experience, every fact has been carefully documented from source materials. Friends at various libraries have been most gracious with their help. Fellow-gardeners and florists have contributed their materials, too. Hubert De Groff Main designed the replica of a classic palette and Thomas A. Turner executed it; to both these talented and busy men, I am greatly indebted. Dorothy Riehm and Elsa Du Puis took over a mass of manuscript which even I despaired of reading once I had written it, and put everything in order. My husband, Laurance Wilson, and mother, Elizabeth Biggin, suffered the usual inconveniences of living with me when I am "up to something," and never complained—bless them.

"Color Photography by Roche" on the title page tells an incomplete story. Mary Alice and Jack Roche are rare friends not only endowed with great talent as photographers but having an uncanny way of divining what you are trying to say before you have even explained your plans. Their studio can always produce a missing prop—even a newly hatched butterfly on one occasion when I wished for an example. Their daughter Deirdre contributed her pet luna moth for a model.

Helen Van Pelt Wilson believed in the ultimate usefulness of this book, and she has been generously forbearing at delays as I waited for new seasons to offer fresh examples for text and pictures. I recall gratefully how often she gave verbal pats of approval on one hand, while with the other—her fine editorial hand—she subdued my ebullient adjectives. I hope her faith is justified.

If I have made any statement you question, I can only answer in the words of Alexander Pope in his *Essay on Man.*

> *All nature is but art, unknown to thee;*
> *All chance, direction, which thou canst not see;*
> *All discord, harmony not understood;*
> *All partial evil, universal good;*
> *And spite of pride, in erring reason's spite,*
> *One truth is clear, whatever is, is right.*

Adelaide B. Wilson

South Orange
New Jersey
September, 1953

1

Color: As We Know It

1

GIFT OF COLOR

Color is one of the shortest words in the language. Its five let-
ters are so familiar that few of us have ever referred to a dictionary for the meaning. Daily papers and periodicals mention
color on almost every page. It is a word which belongs to the
scientist, the artist, the industrialist, and the horticulturist; yet
it is part of everyday idiom, and always understood.

The potential of this word, color, is matched, perhaps, by
only one other word, also a short one—atomic. Both terms stand
for great natural forces which can be made to work for man.
While atomic energy is a force which man must control, color
freely exerts its beneficial power on all our lives. But, like the
atom, color must be understood to be fully appreciated, and it
too should be used with knowledge and discretion. Fortunately
the rules of color are simple, and errors of judgment not catas-

trophic. While we owe most of our knowledge of the nature of color to the scientist, every layman may fully enjoy the gift.

Nature's Colors

To those of us who work with Nature's color in plant materials, there is no richer storehouse from which to choose—nor one more available. As I write, color rushes past my window. An oriole flashes by like a golden streak of lightning, and comes to rest among the branches of a newly-green oak tree. Below us both the garden is radiant with the chromatism of late spring. Silken pink poppies open with dark-blue centers. Early lilies trumpet their brassy intensities. Delphinium grows tall as it matches its blue to the blue sky above. The iris gently compete among themselves and prove their right to be named for the rainbow goddess.

I resist the temptation to gather up all this color and use it for a mass arrangement indoors. By this time I have learned better. These riotous intensities of color in Nature belong in all their glory where the sky is high and soft surrounding greens and shadows modify their showy chromatics. Experience has taught that the gift of color in Nature is not completely mine unless I employ it with discipline.

Color Indoors

In a dimly lighted room, within confining walls, and faced with the rivalry of rugs and draperies and such other of my household gods, Nature's color becomes as temperamental as a prima donna offended by the mimicry of a lesser artist. So, I find I must enjoy rampant color only out-of-doors and inside strive to bring selected hues of flower and foliage into friendly relationship with less versatile manmade pigments.

Perhaps this need for discipline in the use of color is the first lesson for the flower arranger. Lured by the glory of Nature, it is easy for us to forget that color is but one element in the creation of a design. It must be kept in step with the others—form, line, texture, and pattern. Every hue must be chosen with thought of the light in which it will be seen, and of its relation to the space surrounding the finished arrangement. As line and mass set the limits of design, so color must be associated with all other factors. In fact, the secret of using color well lies in respect for many elements—container, component parts, backgrounds. Color is magic, and magic is dangerous without an incantation to protect us from its sorcery.

You recall the story of King Midas whose wish was granted that all he touched should be transformed to gold. He lost his power of choice and only realized his folly when his daughter turned to gold at his kiss. So we may love color but should never surrender completely to its allure. There are rules to be observed, controls to show us where to start and how to stop.

Arranger's Problems of Color

This book is concerned with general concepts of color as they affect flower arrangement which has a problem not common to other forms of art. The painter uses pigments for his pictures, the textile manufacturer works with many dyes. Each starts with fixed elements available in tube or bottle and easily mixed according to need. We must mix our colors with our eyes and with our minds as we create *our* pictures, and we must work with living, ephemeral substances. No flower color is ever fixed. Indeed it is constantly modified as the chemistry of tissues changes, and flowers and foliage fade into successive pigmentations.

With bits of wallpaper and swatches of fabric, we can create a controlled harmony in the living room, but flowers brought from the garden may add beauty today, a note of discord tomorrow. Yellow lilies change to dingy brown; green leaves to yellow. This factor of change makes color in flower arrangement a special delight and also a not-to-be-ignored problem. As we become aware of color as Nature employs it, we tend to get the situation more firmly in hand.

Because plant material is so decorative we accept its transitory loveliness and even put to use its vagaries. I sometimes wait for a flower or leaf to age so that it may attain the elusive color I require. I do not suggest that you use stale flowers, only that you notice the gracious mellowing of petals which often increases the charm of blossoms, as middle age brings greater beauty to many faces.

Sometimes a flower arrangement is in need of a rich bluish-red not often come by in Nature. I have found that the day after the rose Better Times reaches its peak of bloom, it develops a blue shadow in the intense red of the petals which sometimes perfectly suits my purpose. Often a leaf in the prime of life loses its green virility and the resulting mutation makes it a more pleasant companion for the delicate hues with which it is to associate. A dried seed pod, a ghostly preserved flower combined with fresh material may accomplish this same purpose, since dried plants usually become softly grayed. We should be aware of the tricks which natural pigmentation plays and turn them into assets. Your knowledge of plant materials will tell you when anything is too young or too old to retain its condition in a fresh arrangement.

Some time ago I acquired a fabulous pineapple, now the envy of my garden-club friends. Left in a moderately cool place, it was forgotten for months and then discovered dried to the muted gray-white tones of an ancient Roman vase. Enough moisture remained to maintain a feeble life, and the form had shrunk to sculptured beauty. My almost-dead pineapple is an object of admiration whenever I use it. There is no decay, only the graying and maturing which artificial forms do not achieve. I am now experimenting with other fruits hoping to use them as accessories in flower compositions. The textures of living forms seem to me more compatible than most of the bird and beast ceramics or carved figures which we often select for accent notes. (See Plate 6.)

Our Unfailing Source

Color in Nature is an unfailing source of inspiration. Scientific theories and systems offer basic training and color charts lead to a fuller understanding, but Nature remains the finest teacher if her ways are closely observed. The outdoor world offers a palette to the arranger so varied that it is inexhaustible.

In addition to the hues of plants, we have the remarkable coloration of birds and butterflies, even of lowly insects, if we will only be aware enough to examine them. In the Jewel Room at the New York Zoological Garden, which many of us love as The Zoo are tropical birds of such brilliance they out-shine a jeweler's showcase. Hours might be spent there learning lessons in color harmony. From the mineral kingdom came emeralds, amethysts, rubies, and sapphires, whose very names have been applied to many of the spectrum hues. The sea is also a stimulating source for study. Even the less vivid winter woods offer whites and grays and browns with only bits of blue sky or the reddish heads of skunk cabbage introducing shafts of color. Patient lichens breaking up rocks teach their lessons too. When a cardinal in ecclesiastical red perches nearby, a contrast-ing harmony results to inspire a handsome arrangement if we have eyes to see it. (See Plates 3, 7, 11, 15.)

Soon we discover that there are no discordant hues, and that harmony depends upon how we combine them. Science has re-vealed certain truths to help us make our selections. These we can read about in books, and there are also many simple guides for us to follow. But first we must learn to see color with really open eyes—the eyes of the body and the eyes of the mind.

2

THE EYES HAVE IT

Every time the curtains of the eyelids rise, a drama of color unfolds to human sight. The sensation stems from a reaction of the optic nerve so involuntary that we are hardly ever aware that we are seeing color. Yet the experience is as real as a pin prick or the flavor of peppermint on the tongue.

Doubtless it is this effortless ability of the eye to pick up color sensations that makes us almost indifferent to them unless we consciously try to see color more clearly. For most of us the use of color is haphazard and unimaginative. Perhaps when the physical facts of color are better understood we will see it more accurately.

The source of all color is light. The eye receives the light. What then? White light is broken into rays of varying lengths, and it is those broken rays which appear to the human eye as a series of hues. How does the eye sort out the rays? Objects have the power to absorb a number of light rays but generally fail to absorb one. It is this one which is reflected, and this reflected, rejected ray gives a specific color impression, as yellow, or blue, or violet.

Examine the frond of a fern. You see it as green since all but one of the rays derived from white light is beating upon the fern and being absorbed by it. The one which fails to be absorbed is green. Why it happens that way is part of the natural wonder of color. As laymen, you and I can accept this fact gratefully. We need not bother about the scientific explanations which lie perhaps beyond our comprehension.

Perception of Color

For sometime after birth an infant makes no response to color. His stare is almost blind until the day he notices a gleam of light on his rattle and his eyes follow it. His perception of color has begun. Later the child learns the names of his crayons. Now he can identify colors to a degree. He still is not the boy to send to the corner store to match a spool of thread.

Many of us never go beyond such partial identification. All blues look alike. Then one day, perhaps, the distinction between green-blue and violet-blue is recognized. Red is no longer associated only with fire engines; scarlet is distinguished from vermilion or magenta. Gradations of color are more acutely perceived and gradually the eye experiences the rich delight of a wide range of hues.

The physical eye is a wondrously constructed instrument. It is equipped and eager to receive continuous color sensations. But the eye is not satisfied to experience only the one identifiable reflected ray of light which comes from an object. The physical eye actually demands the entire spectrum range of every color sensation.

Stop and think about this almost incredible fact. The eye always demands white light, which is the sum total of all colors. Therefore, although the mind identifies a single hue (as when

the fern was called green), the eye itself is subconsciously adding all the missing colors to that one. When we discuss harmonies, we shall return to this physiological fact as a reason why
certain combinations of colors are especially pleasing.

The Mind's Eye

Color impact upon the physical eye is accompanied by a reaction in the brain. Hue is identified immediately, and any further meaning it may hold calls up other responses. Imagine a
busy street intersection with cars lined up, motors idling. The
traffic signal changes. There is an instantaneous forward surge.
Brakes are released, motors accelerated, all within a split second. Why? Because the stimulus from a green light, plus the
knowledge of what that light stands for, has set up a series of
reactions. Eye, mind, motor nerves all co-ordinate. This commonplace example is typical of the close relationship between
eye and mind.

There may also be an emotional response. Red, white, and
blue on a barber pole has no deeper significance than the green
traffic light. Both are identifying colors. If the same red, white,
and blue appears in an American flag waving before our eyes,
we have a sensation of pride, perhaps an impulse to salute. In
this comparison, we recognize that color not only induces a
physical reaction but that in many instances there is an emotional response. Thus color has a profound effect upon our nervous systems and indeed on our thought processes as well. In addition to the physical aspects of color, there is a psychological
factor which cannot be overlooked.

Bringing this fact down to flower arrangement, we begin to
realize that there are overtones to our color-choice of plant material. A series of relationships is involved—the plants to each
other, to their immediate surroundings, and to our feelings
about them. Orange blossoms, for example, are more likely to
bring to mind a wedding than to suggest their fruit. The
problem may be only a matter of color harmony, or the quality
of design itself may be affected. And beyond the finished ar-

rangement, as something pleasant to look at, is the possibility of a mood to be invoked. Though you may be unaware of such a purpose, if your composition is well executed, it will please more than the eye of the beholder. Judges of a flower show often remark upon the "sensitivity" of an arranger. They mean that without any obvious or artificial accessories to tell a story, a mood has been expressed which brings creator and beholder into sympathetic understanding. To evoke such an emotional response there is no ally like color.

Go into a florist's shop on a wintry February day. Outdoors the wind is whining, the snow swirling. Inside there are yellow daffodils, pink tulips, purple iris, bunches of pansies, and fragrant freesias all about. First you may react to the color, then comes the emotional joy; spring cannot be far away. Go into the same shop in December, poinsettias, carnations, and roses stand among the greens. We call their color Christmas red. Six weeks later a similar mass of red carnations and crimson roses will mean St. Valentine's Day. This is a significance of color which goes far beyond mere identification of hue.

Symbolic and Historic Associations

Emotional response to color is not limited to personal interpretation. All the spectrum hues, with black and white, have symbolic meanings which have been developing for centuries. Today many of the color symbols decreed for the early Christian Church still appear in seasonal usage. It is interesting to learn that color was once employed to present important information which the illiterate had no other means of acquiring. Like the miracle plays which dramatized church history, color pointed up the liturgy—red for the blood of martyrs, green for eternal life.

The historic significance of color is a study in itself. The flower arranger should have at least a superficial knowledge of it. So often schedules for flower shows stipulate a national interpretive arrangement for which arranger and judge need some background. For instance, colors typical of our own

American Indians differ considerably from those of the peoples of eastern Europe or of Africa or even of adjacent South America of the same time. Renaissance colors are opulent and rich; the delicate pastels of the France of Louis XV are chromatically different from the darker hues favored by the court of Louis XVI. Often the most popular colors of a period were the choice of a king's favorite.

Sometimes colors typical of a time and place are a reflection of a foreign influence introduced through discovery and exploration. In our own country the East India trade brought not only different textiles and ceramics but also the hues with which these were dyed or painted. Recently the Williamsburg restoration has inspired us to decorate modern homes with the strong greens and clear yellows of eighteenth-century Virginia. Modern ranch-type houses are decorated in the sandy, dusky-yellow and red-orange values which suggest the southwestern source of their architecture.

A review of traditional color combinations brings inspiration to our work. If we are in danger of becoming safely Victorian in our fearsome use of soft, grayed tones which gave the end of the nineteenth century its name of Mauve Decade, let's look to the long-ago forthright use of colors in Egypt, or the warm strong hues of the Italian primitives.

And the source of this information? The most authentic and available is found in our museums. Even for those who live far from the major collections, there are inexpensive books and numerous reproductions. The Metropolitan Museum of Art in New York offers excellent "miniatures" in faithfully reproduced colors so that anyone may build an historic collection of paintings from the past.

An Eye for Color

"She has an eye for color" is a compliment which suggests an inherited ability to use color well. This is nonsense. Every child has to learn about color the same way although some people seem to develop a seeing eye more easily than others and apparently grow more appreciative of the color sensations inevitable to all humans with normal vision. Actually greater enjoyment is possible for almost all of us who mark well what reaches us through the windows of the eyes.

I cannot remember when I was not keenly aware of color. Although I do not presume to speak as an authority on its scientific aspects, I do consider myself a connoisseur of color since I have spent a lifetime acquiring color experiences. My "collection" started early so that now I can close my eyes at any time and "see" many glowing pictures. These are mine, received with my sight, and held with delight by my mind. I recommend strongly the acquisition of such a repertory of chromatics.

These memories can provide a merciful relief when the physical eye is forced to behold ugliness. That untidy, obese man across from me in the humid subway reminds me of a fat frog in his green suit. Immediately the magic of color has transported me to a cool wilderness tarn; a sapphire bit of sky held like a jewel in the prongs of encircling spruces. A fat frog, his green suit sparkling with the diamonds of the spectrum, grins hospitably from a mossy log. What beauty we have shared in that pool! Refreshed, I open my eyes, and the fat man seems less repulsive. His green suit had worked its color magic on my memory.

Early Awareness

My first recollection goes back to kindergarten where red-letter days were marked by the stringing of gaudy wooden beads on a shoelace. Only two pictures mark those days, the other being the rosy cheeks of a small colleague who for some forgotten reason spent so much time standing in the corner. Perhaps the colorful lure of those beads kept me from being banished to the same spot.

From those days on, my wealth piled up. The dividends have been rich. For me the distant ranges of mountains are not simply brown rocks. At dawn they are delicately pink. Then they rapidly turn to crimson as the sun pushes its way over the peaks.

The long day follows when one value of green after another reflects the sunlight or is darkened by a passing cloud. Toward dusk the mountains deepen to a blue so dark that light seems to have left the range completely. Suddenly the final flare-up of sunlight flushes the opposite ridge with rose, then with red-violet until with a last gallant flourish a great red-orange ball disappears, leaving a violet glow which finally fades to quiet gray.

These are the colors of light, the intangible hues from the palette of the spectrum, a day-long rainbow. I have been personal in recounting all this: color is a personal subject. It is your eye which can see it, your mind which comprehends it. The magic is yours. The eyes have it.

3

GIFT OF LIGHT

We speak of color as a gift. It is one of the greatest and deserves to be dearly held. Humanly we grasp any gift within our reach, eagerly and selfishly. But when the giver is dear to us we see beyond the object itself and are grateful for the thought which went into the selection and the spirit behind the choice. Even the effort which makes a wrapping attractive adds to the meaning of a gift which is accepted not only with the eye and the mind but with the heart. If you and I accept color with such devotion, it will always remain a precious asset in our lives.

Easy Lessons

The average flower arrangement reveals little insight into the bounty of color. Yet within our grasp is pigmentation at its most splendid. Too often plant material is used as if it were but clay or a synthetic derivative. There is a luminosity in the most minute fragment of plant life, a sheen and translucence in every petal to give us a lesson in chromatics.

Study of garden specimens can teach more than all the charts in the world. We need the charts, of course, but only as a springboard for fundamental study. The examination of an individual flower will not necessarily offer an answer to a flower-show schedule, but it will help. A purple pansy with a yellow eye and attending green foliage teaches something, but that does not mean you will win a blue ribbon at the next flower show by entering a green jugful of purple and yellow pansies. The pansy teaches that a speck of intense yellow is as compelling as a larger area of violet, and there is a reason for this. (See Plate 16.) Have you always shuddered at the combination of orange and magenta? But look at the pod of Magnolia macrophylla. See how superbly Nature has combined in it these two most dissonant hues.

We are inclined to take for granted the color which surrounds us today. It beckons from shop windows, from magazine pages, even from the corner fruit stand, and lures us to buy. Modern merchandising has been more alert to the gift of color than we gardeners who work with it in natural form. Perhaps a backward glance will make us more appreciative of what science has done to provide a quicker perception and a more ready guide to understanding color in the decorative arts. Superficial wrappings of emotional response will be torn away to show how wonderful is this gift which is offered.

Scientists have worked for centuries to reveal the mysteries of color that we may see it more clearly and use it more graciously. Our debt to them is considerable and before this book is closed, we shall learn their names and know their contributions. Of course, many will remain anonymous since in the world of science, thousands labor that one may enunciate a truth. Countless workers have picked up the threads of others' efforts and woven a fabric to clothe our ignorance.

A Backward Glance

Early craftsmen had no recourse to paints and dyes in tubes and bottles. They had to find natural sources in tree bark, plants, and insects, even in the soil itself. We may well marvel at the enduring quality of many of the early mixtures. While time has dimmed the colors of some paintings and fabrics, many restorations prove that early Greeks and Egyptians used clear intense hues. There is unmistakable chroma in artifacts thousands of years old.

Primitive man presumably had less perception of color and was content to use the earth hues at hand. Cave drawings which have been found recently bear out this theory. Evidently as man became more creative, he also demanded a wider range of material to express himself. Then there comes a point where visual records disappear and only the tenuous threads of conjecture suggest prehistoric use of color. We know it existed since where there is light there is color; where there were eyes, there was color vision.

Well-documented accounts of evolutionary processes carry the imagination back over millions of years. The seas recede, brown and gray mountains are thrust up. A world of murky darkness appears. It is pervaded with the greenish slime of primeval ooze; from this emerges the one-celled plant, common ancestor of the living world. Records are grayed and sombre, suggesting lower values of color. In this earlier world there is no brilliant glimpse of a butterfly's wing, no lightning flash of a bird in flight, no dynamics of chroma nor the luminosity associated with sunlight.

In working with natural color, as we must do, there is value in retracing this age-old path on which we can see the close relationship between the life of the plant kingdom and the fundamentals of color. Today, when we choose to interpret moods of mystery or sombreness, it is the dark shades of primeval earth that best convey our meaning.

No one has been able to fix a date for the beginning of color on earth. There is a record which carries us back to the vision of its origin. In Genesis, we are struck by the awesomeness of absolute blackness: "And darkness was upon the face of the earth." This phrase denies any gleam of color; there was complete absence of light, a condition which prevented life. "The earth was without form and void." The majestic account rolls on, "And God said, 'Let there be light.'"

The chapter relates how the new existence of plants and animals was assured through the presence of light: "And to everything that creepeth upon the earth wherein there is life, I have given my green herb."

Thus color was born with the gift of light.

4

THEORIES AND SYSTEMS

Two truths have been established at this point: that the source of color is light, and that light rays broken into varying lengths reach the eye and bring to the optic nerve sensations which we identify as color. It has been pointed out that the physical perception of color by the eye is accompanied by an emotional reaction which may be pleasurable or distasteful. While physicists study the problems of light, psychologists explore the effects of color on the nervous system.

Enter the Chemist

A third aspect of research is allied to these two—one which we are inclined to take for granted. This is the chemist's field. Light rays are ephemeral; they cannot be captured for dye-maker or painter. While the physicist can explore and explain the mysteries of light, it is the chemist who must convert color into some tangible form which will paint walls and print textiles. His is the field of pigment.

How many of us as children have watched light coming through a stained glass window and followed with fascination the streamers of color which crossed the room and came to rest in a kaleidoscopic pattern on the floor? Do you recall how we tried to pick up the enchanted hues and were disappointed when our fingers grasped nothing but air? These are the colors of light, intangible, beyond the arranger's control. The colors in the stained glass, however, have substance, for there the chemist has translated the colors of light into pigments.

Color Theories

While these three departments of scientific research—physics, psychology, chemistry—seek facts from the same source, each takes a different path toward the goal. Each field holds certain beliefs and works forward from them with the result that there are three different theories of color and the student is baffled by apparently contradictory concepts. As a result, color appears more difficult to understand than it actually is.

At this point we must distinguish between a fact and a theory. According to the dictionary, a fact is an established truth; it may be accepted literally. A theory is an idea, an explanation, a speculation which, when it has been well conceived, may be accepted for use. For instance, certain natural phenomena can be explained but actual proof of what causes them is not known. Leonardo da Vinci in the late fifteenth century had a theory that man might develop a machine which would fly in the air. His sketches and plans may still be studied. But a flying machine did not become a fact until the Wright brothers built a plane which could remain aloft.

Therefore it is not illogical to acknowledge the validity of all three theories; that of the physicist, of the psychologist, and of the chemist, whose experiments are the basis of the pigment theory. When you are confronted with the differences, remember the story of the blind men who tried to describe an elephant. The first, groping along the sides, said it was firm and broad like a wall. The second, pulling the creature's stringy tail, declared it was like a rope. The third fellow, arm around a staunch leg of the beast, thought it resembled a tree. Each accepted as fact what was really his own theory, limited by blindness and without the perspective of the whole unmistakable bulk of the animal.

The major difference in the three theories lies in what the worker in each field considers the fundamental colors of the spectrum—those hues from which all others are derived.

Physicist's Theory

Since color is derived from white light, it is understandable that the physicist should hold the theory that the most essential colors, the primaries, are those which will add up to white light when mixed in a beam. His primaries are orange-red, green, and blue-violet. The secondary light colors are yellow (with a tendency to orange), blue, and red-violet.

The only concern the flower arranger may have with this theory is in the lighting of a flower show or a special illumination for an exhibit. Few shows at present can afford the luxury of special lighting and, when they can, due to fire regulations, such lights must be installed by a competent electrician. However, we must always be aware of the effect of any light, natural or artificial, upon colors as we use them. For the amateur this is a matter of experience rather than an analysis of the physicist's theory. Therefore, while we may be aware of the implications of the physicist's theory, we need not concern ourselves too deeply with it.

Psychologist's Theory

For the psychologist, color is important as it is received by the eye and reacted to by the nervous system. We have already touched upon the demand of the eye to see all colors at all times. On this fact the psychologist has formulated his theory. For him there are four most important colors, four primaries.

We can satisfy ourselves that his premise is probably true by performing some simple experiments. On a piece of white paper paint a large red disc. Stare at it intently for a few minutes; then close your eyes and relax. On your "mind's eye" will appear a green disc which is the complement of the actual red one you have seen. Or stare at the sun on a bright day. Then close your eyes and you will suddenly "see" behind the closed lids a great violet-blue ball. In each instance the opposite of the perceived color completes the spectrum as demanded by the physical eye.

The phenomenon is known as the "after-image." From the after-image the psychologist reasons that the four basic or primary hues must be yellow, green, blue, and red. The after-image of each seems to satisfy the demands of both eye and mind. It is difficult for us, accepting color so carelessly and casually, to do more than accept these statements as worthy of our attention, leave this theory to the psychologist, and get on with our own problem.

Pigment Theory

The pigment theory brings us laymen to a field in which we can more easily find our way. Accustomed to buying color by the quart, or the yard, or the pound, we find that the pigment theory carries us closer to home, closer indeed than we may think, since we who work with plant materials and natural color must base our study on the chemist's pigment theory. Every gardener knows that plant growth is related to soil chemistry. We recognize the importance of sunlight which permits leaves to manufacture the food which has become available from the soil and water through the root and stem. This botanical House-that-Jack-Built is too familiar to require analysis. Dark days mean poor growth. Plants grown in dense shade lose color and reach desperately for light.

We soon recognize the close analogy of natural chemistry in the garden and synthetics at the chemist's. We gratefully adopt the pigment color theory as our working basis. It is also the standard for most of the decorative arts, as painting, weaving, dyeing.

In the pigment theory, red, yellow, and blue are considered the primaries; orange, green, and violet, the secondaries. In contrast to the colors of light which create white when combined, pigments react in the opposite manner. Mixed together, the primaries approximate black. If two pigment complements are mixed, as red and green, an extremely dark gray is produced.

It is upon this pigment theory that all future references in this book will be based. The color charts we discuss will follow its order. It is most pertinent to the needs of the flower arranger.

The Munsell System

One further point of clarification is needed. Color *theories* are often confused with color *systems*. As color science has developed and color perception increased, the mass of information has almost led to chaos. The situation resembles a house just before a wedding. Packages arrive until the accumulation of boxes and paper and ribbon obscures the gifts themselves. The bride lives in a clutter of teapots and candlesticks. If she had time to think, she might doubt the ultimate usefulness of so much stuff. Later, on the shelves of her new home, she arranges her gifts for use and beauty. She sets up a system.

So systems have been devised to classify colors. As time has brought wisdom, the best of the old systems has been merged with the best of the new and a few excellent patterns have resulted. The one most widely adopted in this country is the Munsell System. This was developed by an American, Albert H. Munsell, an artist and colorist (1858-1918). Although it has not been put to work as yet in the botanical world where we find our medium of expression, we should be acquainted with it in so far as it can help us organize the mass of color facts we need.

The complete pattern of the Munsell System is found in the *Book of Color* which is generally too comprehensive for anyone but a professional colorist. The salient points, as organized by Munsell, are set forth in his small handbook *A Notation of Color*. This should be in the possession of every student. The system has been adopted by the National Bureau of Standards and by a large number of national associations and individuals whose work is concerned with color. Therefore, it is a recommended reference.

Color Dimensions

In Chapter 5, we shall discuss the language of color: hue, value, chroma. The Munsell System is based upon the recognition of these three factors which are referred to as "dimensions." They are used as a yardstick to mark off accurate color intervals by means of numerical symbols. Before entering into the explanation given by Munsell, we must understand fully what these three terms actually represent. Without this well fixed in mind, confusion is inevitable. Simplified as the *Notation* now stands, it nevertheless can be a wilderness in which a novice gets lost.

I would not presume to put into my own words the complicated plan of the system which Munsell and his recent followers have developed, but it may help if the major features are outlined. The student can then explore as she wishes. Here is but a skeleton of the idea. It gives no conception of the immense service and labor which went into the development of this classic work.

Munsell's Hue, Value, and Chroma

First Munsell divided the spectrum into five major color segments—red, yellow, green, blue, purple. We immediately recognize a deviation in interpretation from the six-color pigment spectrum, but we proceed with Munsell. The five majors include an almost endless variety of hues, each at full spectrum intensity, yet possessing discernible differences. For example: Olive green is made of yellow and yellow-green. Its place on a color wheel therefore lies nearer the yellow segment than Nile green which is generally yellow-green, has less yellow, and therefore lies nearer the green segment. Each has distinct characteristics; each is a hue. Perhaps in one segment alone there may be a hundred differing hues between yellow and green which an expert can distinguish.

Value indicates the lightness and darkness which any color may possess, depending upon the amount of white or black which is present. To indicate this graphically, Munsell sets up a vertical column with white at the top, black at the bottom, and an equal mixture of each, called middle-gray or middle-value, halfway up. Each step is identified by number beginning with black at 0, through middle-value at 5, and white at 10. Below 5 we find shades; above 5, tints. You can see how simply this allows you to determine the degree of lightness or darkness of any hue, and call it by number.

Chroma, according to Munsell, is set up with a similar digit identification. Here the steps are measured horizontally. Intense chroma is numbered as high as 18, descending to as low as 0, for something with little color present. A pale pink may have as high a value rating as 9, as low a chroma rating as 3, since there is inherent weakness of color. Royal blue has a high chroma digit; navy blue is low in strength, and therefore rates lower in chroma.

H v/c

This H v/c symbol is used by Munsell to identify any hue, its value, and its chroma; it resembles a mathematical equation and should be memorized. If you remember that value is pictured as vertical, it will become associated with the top symbol of the equation, as v/.

Chroma, graded horizontally, is represented by the lower

symbol /c. Once this fact is retained, it is not hard to follow the equations in Munsell. Let's try one. We find that Y 7/10 means yellow of fairly light value and moderately strong chroma; what we might call lemon-yellow. Or, BG-B 5/6 indicates that if we look at blue-green tending toward blue, reduce its value about half, and note its low chroma, this symbol will probably lead us to a moderately strong turquoise-blue.

When Munsell speaks of "color dimensions" of hue, value, and chroma, he uses a sphere as a graphic symbol of the relationships of the three factors. This sphere resembles a globe with the equator marking the place where spectrum hues are at full chroma. The vertical axis, from north to south pole, represents the value scale with white at north, black at south, and intermediate values between. Middle-gray occurs where the north-south axis crosses the equator. All lighter values or tints are found north of the equator; darker values or shades are south of it. The core of the globe represents the area of grayed hues where color of full spectrum intensity meets the grays and is thereby modified in tone.

Naturally this is not a system to be absorbed in an instant. You and I may never be called upon to put it to use in the flower-arrangement field. However, the Munsell System deserves our respect and recognition.

At present, I understand, there is a beginning toward the simple codifying of colors according to this system. The magnitude of such a project is almost inconceivable, but perhaps a plan will be worked out and we shall some day telephone the florist for carnations R 3/7 and not be surprised at what arrives at the door. In the meantime we can always point a finger at what we want and expect to get it!

The Ostwald System

Many modern colorists base their work on the system originated by Wilhelm Ostwald, a German physicist and Nobel Prize winner (1853-1932).

This system uses as its visual symbol a "double-cone solid."

It is represented by two cones placed base to base with the widest point in the middle and tapering at either end. Immediately there is similarity to the polar regions of the Munsell sphere. However, Ostwald does not mention hue, value, and chroma as qualities of color. Instead he postulates the equation (now called by his name) that "color plus black and plus white equals unity" or oneness. Thus any color plus all the shades, tints, and tones derived from it through the addition of white or black or both expresses the full potential of that color.

Ostwald took an imaginary slice from his double-cone solid and produced a triangle which graphically describes his equation. I suggest that you take a pencil at this point and follow my description. Draw two equilateral triangles base to base. This presents a figure with points top and bottom and broadest where the triangles meet. Label the top angle white, the bottom angle black and connect these with a line. This line is similar to the gray-value scale of the Munsell axis. Spectrum color is found at the widest center line—the equator. Mark the letter C for color at the left-hand angle. Ostwald's slice—his triangle—looked just like the left-hand segment of your drawing with color and white and black forming the three angles. Within the triangle formed by these three marks is unity; within these boundaries are all the possibilities of a color.

Modern colorists find this equation and the Ostwald triangle a simple basis from which they further develop their own interpretations and color systems. Each, moreover, gives to Ostwald full credit for the initial equation and the symbolic triangle. Certain reference books show variations of this triangle in mathematically correct color gradations, a modern improvement which was not available to Ostwald. Industrial uses for such books have led to excellent sources for study although frequently the cost of such books is prohibitive for the average student. However, there are simplified versions which are adequate and helpful in understanding this system.

5

LANGUAGE OF COLOR

Broad understanding of any language brings corresponding pleasure from its written and spoken words. Familiarity gives not only the two dimensions of sight and sound, but also a third, depth, which enriches each word through its context in sentence or paragraph. There are descriptive terms for color which are so generally accepted that, when we hear them, they should invoke instant association with color sensation. Let us not be at a loss in a discourse on color because the terms do not have precise meaning in our minds.

There are two classes of terms—words which belong by birth to color and words which have got into the family through association. For instance, take red. No matter how applied this word has a specific color connotation, as red-hot anger, "seeing red," Reds as a political group. Red is closely identified as a color name, a surname, which suggests fire, heat, brilliance, dynamics.

Then we have a word like tone. For the music student, tone is associated with sound. To the fashion editor, it conveys something different. The colorist uses tone to indicate deviation from a spectrum color. We speak of tones of green or yellow, brown or blue. Sometimes we apply tone to a spectrum hue, but in a more exact use tone indicates any modification which involves graying. The various interpretations of this word have been accepted somewhere, sometime, in the art world. It is therefore not for us narrowly to restrict its use. Tone is one of the words which belongs to the color family by adoption.

Spectrum Terms

The nomenclature of color is now examined not alphabetically but, to my mind, logically, as in the presentation of a cast of characters—in order of appearance. For clarification, brief program notes are given. Remember the viewpoint is that of the pigment theory.

SPECTRUM. Colors visible when white light is broken into rays of various lengths as it passes through the atmosphere. The natural spectrum appears in the rainbow when the light of the sun comes splintered and refracted through moisture in the air. A spectrum can be produced by passing a ray of light through a glass prism. The resulting refraction will show a rainbow band on a white paper. The same effect is approximated when the sun shines on spray from the garden hose. (See Plate 1.)

SPECTRUM COLORS. The six most distinctive in the spectrum —red, orange, yellow, green, blue, and violet. In the spectrum band these do not appear as separate units, each in a box, but as neighboring hues that merge, and in merging create other colors. These intermediates may be countless but our imperfect perception limits the number we can identify. The eye which is color-conscious distinguishes more than the unreceptive and untrained eye. Keep in mind this idea of a continuing band of color; then the apparent deviations in color charts will be easier to comprehend.

PRISMATIC COLOR.   Synonymous with Spectrum.

PRIMARY SPECTRUM COLORS.   (Pigment Theory.)   Red, yellow, blue, so called because they cannot be broken down into other hues. Mixed in pigments, they produce a pigment apparently, but not absolutely, black. This imperfection is the result of impurities in most pigments. (The light primaries differ and are considered to be those hues which when added together in three rays of light become pure white light.)

SECONDARY SPECTRUM COLORS.   Made by mixing two pigment primaries as: orange, produced by red plus yellow; green, produced by yellow plus blue; violet, produced by blue plus red. You will find that some charts and references substitute purple for violet in naming this spectrum secondary. Purple is also used to denote a mixture in which there is more red than blue. Hence, violet is a more accurate term here.

TERTIARY SPECTRUM COLORS.   Made by mixing a primary and a secondary. The names suggest the origins: red-orange, yellow-orange, yellow-green, blue-green, blue-violet, red-violet. Note that the primary is mentioned first and that the mixture of equal amounts is indicated by the hyphen as in red-orange. Mixtures of unequal amounts are indicated as in reddish-orange or red red-orange. This denotes a hue dominantly red-orange but with a preponderance of red. Greenish-yellow or yellow green-yellow is dominantly yellow but with some green added.

Exactness of nomenclature is most important. Yet many of these hues have been given other names which sound delightful and alluring, but are often misleading. Peach color is used to denote a tint of orange, and is usually so understood. Actually a peach can be green or yellow or almost red, depending on variety or ripeness. Chartreuse is a casual descriptive term for yellowish-green. Named after the liqueur, chartreuse as used in advertising describes almost anything between yellow and green. Plum has general acceptance as dark purple-red, but there are green and yellow-green plums as well as those which are purple.

All these are color terms by association, widely understood and accepted as adequately descriptive. I have used them in this book when speaking in general terms. For complete accuracy in flower-show work use spectrum names to identify all hues. This applies particularly to making and interpreting schedules for shows.

One further point, spectrum hues, whether primaries, secondaries, tertiaries, or further admixtures, are colors at full saturation with neither black nor white added. A spectrum yellow may appear less intense than spectrum red but both are at peak of power.

Qualities of Color

All colors possess three distinct qualities or attributes. The Munsell System is based on this.

HUE. Almost a synonym for color; defines a sensation which reaches the eye regardless of how light or dark it is; for example, pink, turquoise, navy, cream, or eggplant are hues although they are either lighter or darker than spectrum colors.

VALUE. Lightness or darkness of any hue, indicates the presence of white or black or both as in a "grayed" color. Value is possibly the most useful asset of color. Change in value allows wide variation when only one hue is used. A grayed color with its balanced tonality is always pleasant.

TINTS. Spectrum colors mixed with white; also called high or light values.

SHADES. Spectrum colors mixed with black; also called lower or dark values.

TONES. Grayed-values of spectrum colors.

Tints, shades, and tones are terms used very flexibly in common parlance. We have stockings in "shades of beige" which are obviously lighter than spectrum hues. Look at the array of dark red nail polish in a drug store. Calling these "various tints of red" is not accurate; they are light, dark, or grayed-reds. It is good practice thus to refer to value of colors as lighter, or darker, or grayed rather than as tints and shades and tones. (See Plate 6.)

CHROMA. Intensity or strength of hue. Spectrum hues are of full intensity, as saturated with color as possible, although some appear less strong than others. The distinction between value and chroma often bewilders students because it appears that in both instances color is modified. Chroma has nothing to do with a hue being lightened or darkened in value. *Its intensity is an inherent quality* which distinguishes between a strong color and a weak one.

Distinctions may be compared to the C notes up and down a piano keyboard. High C may have a thinner sound than middle C, and bass C may have greater depth. But all are the same note with varying intensities of pitch. There may be six blues each at fullest saturation of blue-ness, yet one will have stronger chroma in comparison to any other.

In the garden, a planting of tulips, Red Emperor, may stand beside a clump of daffodils, King Alfred. Both have color at almost full-spectrum chroma. The tulips appear more intense than the daffodils because of the greater chromatic strength of their red. An adjacent planting of violets covers more space but appears less strong, though of spectrum intensity. This is because violet inherently has less impact of chroma than red or yellow.

Hue, value, and chroma are modifying influences which make color more usable. Exposure to intense red over a period of time could build up nervous tension to the point of madness, certainly to uncontrollable irritation. Too much spectrum blue might be depressing enough to induce melancholia. Yellow staring us in the eye with no relief tends to produce sun-blindness. We need to know and employ to their fullest the three modifying qualities of color. We will go into this further when we come to color harmonies.

NEUTRAL COLORS. Black and white do not appear in the spectrum. We know that white is the source and sum of all color.

What about black? In Genesis it signifies absence of light. The dark velvet of a moonless and starless night can seem black, but actually, there is some light present. Yet it is difficult to walk in a woodland on such a night, crashing into trees, and not believe that we are experiencing total darkness. Black is the antithesis of light and not a color at all. Long ago artists found that they needed a pigment which would indicate light, and also its absence, so white and black were added to the palette of pigments. Today we consider them as colors but call them neutrals.

Neither pure white nor absolute black appears in the plant world. The plants which most reasonably might be called white are the saprophytes like Indian pipe which show almost no vestige of color. Yet in sunlight, they too reflect certain hues. Gardenias and magnolias are almost white yet hold a trace of color. The famous black tulip which created history as well as hysteria in Holland was not truly black. These so-called white or black flowers are actually of neutral colors.

Neutral colors, therefore, are those which are so reduced in value and chroma that they possess no identifiable spectrum color. The sand of the seashore appears grayish-white, apparently a true neutral, but let a handful run through your fingers in the sunlight and the rainbow appears in miniature. A piece of slate may be so dark a grayish value as to be classified as neutral, but let a ray of sunlight slant across the slab, and again there is a revelation of spectrum color.

Neutral colors make excellent backgrounds, and they are good transition values, giving respite from the full intensity of more clearly defined hues. Light neutral colors are found upon analysis to be spectrum hues so reduced in value that they are almost white, but with enough black added to give a grayish tonality. Likewise, a very dark neutral color can appear so black that only the presence of a little white reveals its spectrum origin.

NEUTRALS are white and black and the grays which result from mixing the two. The equal mixture of white and black pigment produces middle-value or medium-gray. From this central point, going in either direction, lighter or darker grays are achieved. These are called *grayed-values* and are not to be confused with the *grayed colors* we just discussed.

Why do we make this distinction between the two classes of neutrals and neutral colors? Because, while the plant world includes many neutral colors, true neutrals are as nonexistent as true black or white. The artemisias and some of the sedums and cacti appear gray, but inspection and comparison with an inorganic pigment gray reveals that even these plants possess a degree of color.

While we have no neutrals among plants, flower-show schedules sometimes require an arrangement which suggests twilight or restraint, or an arrangement in grayed values. The arranger may do a careful job, painting a container with a mixture of black and white and selecting soft grayed plant material, reduced in value, but the result is flat, ugly, and rather grim. Had she used neutral colors for her paint, that is, colors which contained the basic spectrum hues of the plant material she had chosen, there might have been a sympathetic blending of tonalities. Good grays are made by mixing complementary colors, and then adding white. Watch any expert decorator at work; it is a revelation to discover what pigments he put into the mixing of a pleasing neutral color.

WARM COLORS. Red, orange, and yellow, as in one section of the spectrum, so named because of association with fire, heat, radiance, sunlight. Also called "advancing colors," as they seem to move quickly toward the eye. (Also known as xanthic colors.)

COOL COLORS. Green, blue, violet, as in one part of the spectrum. These suggest cool shade, distant skies, deep shadows. Called also "receding colors" because they appear to withdraw from our vision. (Also known as cyanic colors.)

It is interesting to notice that yellow and violet can join either group. Yellow used with the red and orange segments of a color wheel takes on their vibrancy, but yellow in conjunction with the greens and blues loses its effect of warmth in their recessiveness. This makes yellow a most useful color always, as we shall see later in considering harmonies. Likewise, violet moving in with the reds, assumes a warmth which is quite different from the coolness of violet when used with the blues.

We have now assembled a handful of word-tools to help us dig more deeply into the meaning and use of color. With these few guides we can define color for our needs and interpret color problems with more accuracy. To say we want a dark value of green with an accent of intense red may bring to mind a holly tree with its bright berries, or a mass of scarlet geraniums against a background of yews. The lovely lyrical names of topaz and turquoise, champagne and sherry are only acceptable when we speak of colors in a general way. More exact terminology is required in setting up and in solving the specific problems of flower arranging.

6

MAKING COLOR CHARTS

The study of color requires the guidance of a reliable color chart. Such a visual aid is an ever-ready reference which often answers a question with a glance. A chart gives a complete picture of the spectrum relationship with values and intensities in organized form. There are many excellent charts available at low cost, and the wise student will own several for their differing approaches to a basic problem.

It is these varying viewpoints, however, which often confuse the novice. Color charts do not always agree in their presentation of the subject. Their color identification is frequently difficult to reconcile with what we believe is spectrum intensity. Ownership of two divergent charts may lead to doubt of the authenticity of both or tempt you to lean heavily on one.

Either way is dangerous. There may be discrepancies in the

mechanical reproduction of the colors. Pigment colors are not always accurately shown by printer's ink which is transparent and therefore less effective than an opaque paint. Inferior paper or one unsuited to color reproduction may distort the intention of a chart of color. Therefore it behooves us not to depend explicitly on any one projection of color. Accept the benefits of several charts, but use such aids only as guides, not vehicles. No map can carry you to a specified place but it can show a way for you to travel there under your own power.

The perfect color wheel could be made, perhaps of carefully matched and mounted samples, each chosen with scientific accuracy. The cost of producing such a guide would make it prohibitive for the average person, so it is best for us to use what we have with a tolerance which will prevent our own viewpoint from becoming inflexible. The custom-tailored chart is not an impossibility, and the student will do well to construct her own.

There is satisfaction in seeing what goes into the mixing of the more complex hues. A little working with pigments provides an experience more valuable than hours of abstract theorizing. Even a layman knowing little of the artist's techniques can make a useful chart with water-color paints. Such a guide, of course, should be supplemental to a professional chart, most of which are designed to be mathematically precise. Many paint companies provide these as part of their consumer service, and employ expert technicians to devise them.

The homemade chart has merit because colors come direct from pigment and not secondarily as through a printing process. For years I have used a set of charts which I made to fit into a pocket-sized notebook. They have been invaluable. I still make charts from the true colors which can be bought in opaque paints. The process is simple, the results rewarding.

The Essentials

OPAQUE PAINTS. These are sold under brand-names at artists' supply stores. Your local stationer or paint-dealer will doubtless have them too. They are also known as poster paints or tempera (the latter being not too accurate a term). They may be acquired in sets, or separately, each jar a color of spectrum intensity and amazingly accurate. They are soluble in water and when used as already mixed in the jar will cover any paper with an opaque coating. Sets usually include the six spectrum colors, although some have tertiaries too. Cost is relatively low, and usually complete sets include a good color chart for reference.

BRUSHES.   Three small ones such as artists use. These need not be first quality, anything which does not shed hairs will serve the purpose.

PAPER.   The best choice is an 8- by 11-inch pad for water colors. Any paper used with poster paints must have a finish which is suitable for water colors. White is best for this purpose.

POSTER CARDBOARD.   Two sheets for mounting colors. Good size is 20 by 30 inches.

COMPASS.   Since charts are usually designed in a circle, you need a compass to draw a perfect circumference. However, a dinner plate or any large unit for the wheel, plus glass tumblers in varying sizes for the color units, will do equally well.

SCISSORS AND PASTE.   To mount color circle on the wheel.

MUFFIN TIN.   The several cups of a muffin pan filled with clean water help you to avoid mixing the colors when you clean brushes. Water should be replaced often to prevent muddying fresh paint as you dip the brushes.

MEDICINE DROPPER.   For measuring pigment.

CLOTHS.   Clean cloths for wiping brushes to avoid saturation with either water or paint; colors must be kept clear.

TIME.   Three or four hours, preferably when daylight is good and there is no need for artificial lighting which alters color.

Procedure

The tools just listed allow us to prepare a number of colored papers in true spectrum chroma. From these, we can cut out

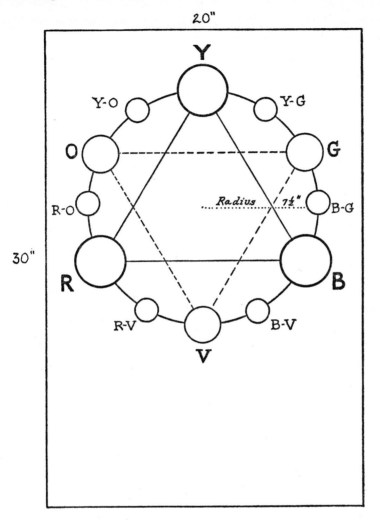

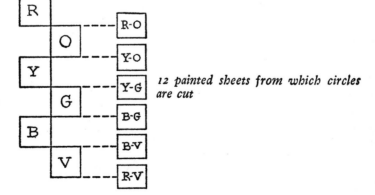

12 painted sheets from which circles are cut

sections to place at proper intervals in a circle for a wheel of twelve hues, including primaries, secondaries, and tertiaries. A wheel of this extent is sufficient for our modest needs. A large chart can be made first; the leftover scraps will provide a pocket-sized set.

The size of the chart depends on your need. I have found one built on a 20- by 30-inch poster board provides units large enough to be easily seen. I prefer a twelve-hue circle. In addition, I set up a separate sheet for each color and its light and dark values. The wheel and the sheets are not too complicated for a novice to manage. So, first, we shall plan the color circle alone.

Tear twelve sheets of paper from the painting pad. Have your brush clean and not too wet. Moisten it with clean water. Then dry it sufficiently so that there is no dilution of the paint.

Begin with the three primaries—yellow, blue, and red—cover each paper with one color. Make brush strokes broad enough to apply color evenly. The result should show no streaks or variance of chroma or value. Set these three sheets aside to dry. At first they will appear shiny but will ultimately have a mat finish, true to the spectrum.

Next paint three sheets with the secondaries—orange, green, and violet. While you wait for the six basic hues to dry, experiment with color mixing. This time mix your own secondaries— orange, by combining red and yellow; green, by combining yellow and blue; violet, by combining blue and red. See how closely you have come to matching the commercially prepared pigments. This is an excellent way to distinguish strength and weakness of chroma. You will find that some paints seem to possess less force and intensity than others although all are at full spectrum saturation.

Prepare the next six sheets of paper for the tertiaries. If your paint set includes these ready-mixed, this will be simple. Once again while these are drying, try mixing your own tertiaries to study their composition. This time you will find it a little more difficult to be accurate since in this mixture three hues are involved. Red-orange, derived from red and orange, actually includes red, orange, and yellow; blue-green is based on a combination of yellow, green, and blue; and so on.

I cannot underestimate the value of making your own color mixtures even when a commercial chart of unmistakable merit is at hand. While reading recipes for a new dessert or tasting someone else's cooking stimulates eye and palate, the knowledge and satisfaction of personal achievement is missing unless you too concoct the same delicacy.

Making a chart increases your perception so that you are aware of the slightest digression as when one hue becomes ever so little dominant in a mixture. Mixing tertiaries will possibly lead you further than you planned to go. You may come up with a red, red-orange which goes beyond the limits of even a tertiary mixture. To be able to perceive and to rectify any mistake in matching what you have mixed with paint from the bottle is a step toward eye-power.

Assembling the Chart

Now you have twelve pages of spectrum hues, also a poster board. On this draw a circle with a diameter of 15 inches. Make three small circles with your compass or draw around drinking glasses of three slightly different diameters; say 3 inches, 2½ inches, and 2 inches. Stemmed glasses are easy to handle.

With the colored side face-down, to protect the paint in case of error, draw a circle on each of the sheets of primary color. Use the largest glass or set your compass at 1½ inches. Use the next smaller glass to outline a circle on each secondary-color sheet, and the smallest glass for the tertiaries. When these circles are cut out, the various sizes make identification of the three groups of hues easier.

If you wish to be minutely accurate and are versed in geometry, divide the 15-inch circle on the poster cardboard into three equal parts with a compass. If you are casual, like myself, draw an equilateral triangle, approximately 13 inches to a side on the 15-inch circle. It will divide it neatly. At the apex, place yellow; at the lower right angle, blue; at the lower left angle, red.

Lo, the primaries are in position! When evenly spaced, they can be pasted down.

We might digress here to note that there is no right or wrong placement of the primaries. No circle has beginning or end, and neither has the spectrum. But it is helpful to establish a fixed spot where you can always expect to find a primary hue. Since yellow and violet are the dividing line between warm and cool colors, it seems wise to give them a vertical position. Then each half-circle holds these psychological groupings.

In placing the secondaries, reverse the triangle. Put violet opposite yellow, green opposite red, orange opposite blue. When six small circles are pasted down, the basic spectrum is completed. All further colors will be the admixtures. Proceed to add the tertiaries halfway between their constituent parts; red-orange between red and orange, and so around.

Perhaps by this time you will be carried away with your project and, while the painted papers are drying, you will continue to mix new combinations just to see what happens. All kinds of surprises lie in store. Remember that even now, the black and white pigments have remained unopened; all painting so far has been limited to hues of full spectrum intensity. Mix red and green and see what evolves. Try blue and green, or yellow and violet. The more experimenting the greater your eventual understanding of color terms.

I recall a sad experience at a flower show. The class called for a monochromatic composition and my entry was based upon orange. The container was a grayed-brown, the leaves dark brown, the flowers ranged from light values of orange to an accent of pure chroma. All trace of another color had apparently been eliminated which is not always possible in creating a monochrome. The judges spent more time than seemed necessary discussing the arrangement. Someone later reported that they questioned the brown leaves, not recognizing this hue as a shade of orange. Had any one of them ever made a color chart, she could have come to a quicker decision. The arrangement won no ribbon: "The judges failed to consider it monochromatic." Ah, me!

Preparing the Value Chart

The simplest exposition of color values can be planned within a rectangle. Procure a second cardboard, and this time use the long dimension horizontally. Allow a margin of 2 inches top and bottom; a margin of 3 inches at either side, and draw a rectangle within the margins. It will measure 24 by 16 inches. Divide the rectangle horizontally at intervals of 2 inches; vertically at intervals of 4 inches. Now you have the spaces in which the colors and their light and dark values can be placed.

LIGHT VALUES (Tints).   The spectrum hues are already provided for, these having been left over from the circles cut for the wheel. In this operation, the tertiaries will be omitted and only the six basic spectrum hues will be lightened.

Put a small amount of spectrum hue into six separate cups of your clean muffin tin. These furnish convenient receptacles for mixing. Finish working with one color before starting on another but allow the same amount of white for each hue with

Making a Value Chart

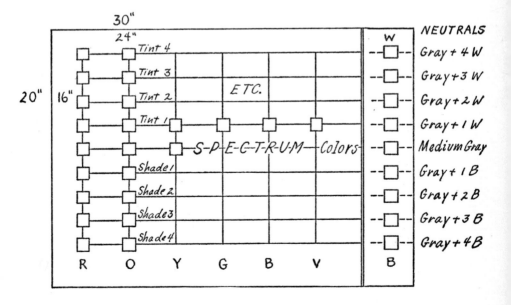

which you work. Use a medicine dropper to control the amount of white added at each step.

Use two sheets of paper for every hue. Then paint half of one sheet with the first tint, adding four drops of white to the pure hue. Double the amount of white each successive time. There will be a perceptible change in value, each step becoming lighter. (There is no way to give explicit amounts since each of you will have a different technique. By using your own judgment, the result will be satisfactory if you are careful to add the same quantity of white at every step and for every color.) If you increase the white four times, you will provide four tints of each hue.

DARK VALUES (Shades). Before proceeding, be careful to have all brushes and the muffin tins completely clean, free from any trace of white. Only then is it safe to repeat the procedure, this time adding black instead of white. Begin once again with the six spectrum hues. Start with the addition of only two drops of black. Black pigment has a tendency to darken quickly, and the steps which create tints may move toward a very dark value too quickly to maintain a hue identity. Once again you must use your own judgment, experimenting with one of the hues before working with all.

Darkening will be more perceptible than when white was added. Black pigment is made up of different elements and sometimes tends to introduce another hue. You will be astonished at what happens to yellow at about the second step. Unless you have had this experience, it is difficult to pass judgment on the work of one more expert in color. For instance, even a slightly darker value of yellow appears olive-green. Many persons unfamiliar with this fact misjudge a monochromatic which includes this value with a yellow scheme.

Assembling the Value-Chart

When all painted papers are thoroughly dry, prepare chips or pieces of each spectrum hue at full chroma and for each value by cutting out 2-inch squares. Start at the center horizontal line. Place the six hues in order, beginning with red so that they form a spectrum band, each halfway down the vertical column. Add light values in ascending scale, and dark values in a descending scale in each column, above and beneath the spectrum hue. When all are correctly placed, paste chips so that there appears a continuous vertical scale of each hue with a margin separating it from the next color.

Neutrals

Since black and white are considered pigment colors (not spectrum hues, however), it is proper to include their value-scale also. Paint one sheet of paper half white and half black. Mix equal amounts of both to get medium-gray which is called middle-value. In two muffin cups put small amounts of medium-gray. To one cup add white four times, doubling the amount each time, just as was done with spectrum colors. Likewise, add black to the other cup in the same ratio to develop darker values of gray.

In the right-hand margin of cardboard which shows color values, place the neutrals as follows: Opposite the center line place medium-gray; at the top, place white; at the bottom place black.

Fill the intervening spaces with lighter and darker values in order. Note that these neutrals are placed in the margin and not within the rectangle itself. This is done to avoid confusion between the spectrum tints and shades and the neutrals. The addition of gray to any hue produces a quality which is usually called a tone.

There is another device which I recommend to you. This is a book of color swatches prepared commercially in the exact spectrum hues with their light and dark values. The one I use constantly, compiled by Sidney Beller, is called Color-aid. This is a book 5 by 3 inches containing over two hundred swatches; twenty-four hues of spectrum intensity with tints and shades of each; also eight values of gray. Each sample is identified. In checking the colors for the plates in Part Three, I have used these swatches to authenticate the colors described there. See the reference list on page 121 for a source for Beller's book.

Charts can be made using pages from this book, but I still recommend that you also learn color by mixing your own pigments.

Moral

Does all this hold anything pertinent to flower arranging? I refer you to the sad little story of the judges who did not know where brown had its beginning.

2

Color: As We Use It

7

HARMONIES OF COLOR

The rainbow in the sky with its full complement of intense chroma is one of Nature's most inspiring spectacles. Yet the same colors combined in fabrics or flowers often look garish, even offensive. There is a difference between the colors of light and those of pigment. The colors of light are translucent; pigment, spreading over surfaces, is opaque and substantial. The rainbow colors reach the eye through long veils of atmosphere; the colors of the things we touch are viewed nearby.

An analogy might be made with dancers seen on a stage from an orchestra seat. The corps de ballet is pink-cheeked and smiling. Powerful lights cast a luminous glow. The staging is cunningly designed for the distance between audience and dancers. Backstage and close-up under the stark reality of a single electric bulb the heavily pigmented mouths and cheeks and eyes appear grotesque. The make-up man has been aware of the power of *both* his pigment color and that of the lighting. With knowledge and skill he has used his colors expertly. Light and space and careful modulation of color have produced harmony to charm the spectator.

The rainbow is proof that there are no truly inharmonious colors since all have their beginning in white light and possess a basic relationship. It also shows that there is an orderly progression from red through violet. We may learn from this. The eye is an arbitrary organ which chooses to recognize this order; the mind accepts the color combinations as pleasing. Such organized relationships are called color harmonies.

Related and Contrasted Harmonies

The most appealing combinations fall into two categories; related colors and contrasted colors. Study the differences with a color chart in hand. There are two related harmonies, the monochromatic and the analogous. Contrasts result from those hues which are directly opposite. These are called direct complements. They proceed through several modifications of this opposition, as split complements, triads, double split complements, tetrads, and others still more complex. Let us consider first their points of similarity between related and contrasted harmonies.

Many colorists believe that related harmonies which are adjacent on the color wheel have a great emotional appeal, and that the contrasts which lie farthest apart satisfy the eye most fully. Such distinctions seem artificial at first, but there is good reason to accept them.

In a related harmony, the eye travels over a small area. Therefore there are no disturbing jumps, no sudden contrasts. For instance, we find that green, green-yellow, and yellow, the colors of spring forsythia and daffodils, present a related harmony which is easy to accept. The mind remains placid; it is not over-stimulated.

On the other hand, that most wonderful instrument, the eye, is not so easily pleased since no single ray of color satisfies it. If the eye sees green, it must also see the other hues of the spectrum. The eye is constructed to receive white light and, in perceiving but one hue, subconsciously it must see all the rest of the rainbow. Contrasting harmonies are therefore more satisfactory to the eye for they provide the full scope of the spectrum. The eye actually is allowed to see in contrasts all the color it so eagerly desires. The mind confronted with contrast might be imagined as saying: "It is all very well for you to hop from side to side of a color chart, but for me, let me take it step by step without so much effort."

This business of emotional (mind) versus physical (eye) color reaction is important to consider when you are combining colors. Why? Because in making arrangements you are endeavoring to please yourself or some onlooker, even a judge! You may be trying to evoke a mood or an emotional response.

Never forget that the physical response to color actually can produce eye-weariness, if contrasts are too sharp and too insistent. Related color harmonies can be compared to close friends who are so congenial that we rejoice in their easy companionship and feel no compulsion to entertain them. Contrasts on the other hand are as stimulating as interesting strangers. We cannot sit by and be unaware of them.

Origin of Principles of Harmony

Before proceeding, we must acknowledge the great debt we owe to the man who co-ordinated these truths and established them as principles for us to follow. They are all carefully defined and explained in *The Principles of Harmony and Contrast of Colours* by Michel E. Chevreul. Early in the eighteenth century, Chevreul was director of the wool-dyeing at the great Gobelin tapestry-works. It was his job to produce colors so well related to each other that in the weaving there would be no lack of harmonious blending. His problems of combining various colors and their infinite variety of values were not easily solved. He discovered that identically colored wools, the products of the same dye-pot, look different according to the hues next to them.

This led to the discovery that colors actually react upon each other when placed in juxtaposition; that two directly contrasting hues of equal intensity make each other appear even more intense. Chevreul stated this as "the law of simultaneous contrast," and it would be impossible to overestimate its importance. To him we owe the concept of related and contrasted harmonies. (See Plates 8. and 10.)

Our problems in flower arrangement are similar to Chevreul's in tapestry: how to combine colors of plant material so there will be harmony and beauty to please both the eye and the spirit.

No one can adequately appreciate Chevreul's contribution unless this great book of his is read. Written originally in French but available in translation, it is not easy reading but worth the respectful attention of anyone who would learn about color. Here is the experience of a scientist who loved color, who worked with it continually, and who formulated from a mass of experiments a few simple facts. No one can tell Chevreul's story as he does. His style is quaint and rather ponderous, but it has a courtly flavor which is delightful. If much of this large book proves too technical, at least skim through it and capture some of its rich essence. If I could own but one color reference, this would certainly be my "desert island" choice.

8

MONOCHROMATIC

The word monochromatic defines this harmony: one-color. A single hue of the spectrum limits the range. There can be no deviation to the right or to the left on the color wheel. Should red-orange be the choice, red and orange have no place in the harmony even though they are the components of the hue. Actually they are different colors and must not be included. This harmony calls for a scrupulous fidelity to the chosen color. You may ask if such a single hue can be made into an interesting composition or will it result in monotony. The answer in either case may be yes, but well handled a monochrome can be dramatic and far from monotonous.

To accomplish this, it is essential to make use of all the assets of value and chroma in the hue. You can see that this widens the range considerably. With the red-orange, for instance, values may include not only the lighter tints we call peach and melon and salmon, but also the deep-bronze and red-brown shades. Add to these the muted, grayed red-orange tones, and the scope becomes evident.

To add interest to a monochrome, elements of texture and form should be considered. The smooth weightiness of bronze is well contrasted with the textural roughness of branches. Spikes of tall flowers contrast well with globular forms. Sizes may vary. We know that color without support from other elements of design can prove woefully inadequate. So often a monochrome is approached with only the intense spectrum hue in mind. You can appreciate its potential only when these other factors are taken into consideration.

Visual Weight

This is a good place to introduce a new power of color, the illusion we call "visual weight." While a red rose and a pink one might weigh the same on a scale, the red one will always give the appearance of being heavier. A stalk of yellow gladiolus will never seem quite so strong as a similar stalk of red-violet. Dark colors always appear heavier, light ones less substantial. We can never minimize the factor of visual weight. It is especially important when you work with a monochrome.

A jump from a very light value to a dark one with no gradual transition will appear contrasting rather than related. The charm of a monochrome lies in its unity. The eye and mind both are pleased when movement from light to dark is orderly. If there is one single lesson to be learned when planning a monochrome, perhaps this is it.

Let us return to the chosen red-orange. An arrangement could be made of the most delicate peach stock with deeper-hued gladiolus, the whole brought together with salmon poppies. All this material lies in the area of lighter values which never touch full spectrum chroma. Or the choice might lie below the middle-values. Dark red-brown leaves of flowering cherry could support dahlias of a lighter shade. A third variation might involve grayed-values of dried materials with a brilliant cluster of red-orange cockscomb introduced at full-spectrum chroma. These three simple examples have, you may notice, not only drawn upon values and chroma but have suggested a variety of forms and textures also.

Opportunity of the Monochromatic

The monochromatic is always a *safe* harmony. It is frequently the answer to a decorating problem in a room where figured draperies and wallpaper have already introduced such a range of color that a flower arrangement is only likely to add further confusion. Here a bold dramatic monochrome picking up a dominant color could easily steal the scene. In a dull uninteresting room such a focal point of plant material provides real drama. In a crisp, sophisticated room, a serene monochrome speaks with a gentle authority, perhaps through a single sweeping branch with a color at the base echoing the draperies. Always remember that contrast of pattern is also a tool for us to use.

In the modern decorator's idiom, monochromes are used almost too often. Stark, sleek interiors are so limited in color and so dependent on texture for interest that they offer opportunity for the flower arranger to play a stellar role. With background color so subdued that it is difficult to identify the exact hue, the wise arranger points it out and relieves its anonymity with intense spectrum color.

Flower shows often provide drab, uninspired backgrounds for exhibits with the hope that all the exhibitors will thus find happy homes for their many-hued arrangements. Even here a smart monochrome can have its place. After a riot of chroma, the subtly conceived monochrome will attract the tired eyes of the judges with psychological cleverness. Closely associated tonalities are like a merciful cloud over a summer sun.

About Foliage

One further question looms, specifically in the province of the arranger—what about foliage? How can a monochromatic harmony be strictly maintained when there are leaves and stems of green or some other hue? When the schedule of a show says "other foliage permitted" there is some freedom. Even so, the cautious arranger will choose materials most faithful to the single hue. There are colored leaves other than green, and stems of brown, or red, or yellow, yes, even of blue, as in Salvia farinacea. Material and container can be selected so that off-color elements are eliminated. The seeing eye must sternly discriminate so that little visibility is allowed any other color present.

All of which brings up the fact that while inorganic pigments can be obtained to produce a monochromatic harmony, this is not possible in the plant world. Just as there is no truly white or black plant, there is, so far as I ever have been able to discover, no completely monochromatic flower or leaf or fruit. There are many which apparently fill the need, but scrutiny inevitably fastens upon veins or stamens or centers of distinctly different hues. Nature presumably does not approve of monotones and adds an alien touch regardless of manmade laws of color harmony. Therefore, it behooves us not to try to change her ways or to make flower-show schedules so inflexible they are not realistic. (See Plate 4.)

I have been present when exhibitors and judges have wasted valuable time trying to gainsay these natural facts. Often the beauty of an arrangement has become secondary to a zeal for achieving a monochromatic scheme. It seems incredible, but I once heard a speaker recommend that the eye be plucked out of pansies to eliminate the contrasting center, that tweezers were the tool for tearing stamens from lilies when they failed to measure up to the demands of a color class. Such mutilation is unforgivable. Anyone who perpetrates such outrages should be limited to poison ivy for her exhibits. The miracle of every flower is too exquisite for us to dare to intrude.

The monochrome, therefore, must be the result of a conscientious effort on the part of the arranger to make her point while disciplining her own eye for color, and not wreaking her frustration on the innocent bloom itself.

9

ANALOGOUS

The analogous group of harmonies is most frequently misunder-
stood. It is true that there is more than one interpretation of
what exactly defines its limits but there is a boundary which is
generally accepted in the decorative arts, and should be accepted
by arrangers as well. Let us first be sure we understand the
term; flower-show schedules too often employ it carelessly.

Analogous is one of those words which the colorist has taken
from general nomenclature and then given a particular meaning
in his field. The dictionary defines analogous as having resem-
blance but not being the same. It is a kinship, a link, which in
some way binds two or more identities otherwise disparate.
Perhaps we might say that a twin brother and sister are analogous; they have a blood relationship but a distinction in sex and
possibly appearance. What about analogous colors?

Actually all spectrum colors are analogous because they are derived from white light and have a basic kinship, but this is too wide an interpretation to be useful. It is accepted practice to limit an analogy to that section of the color wheel which contains but one pigment primary. Refer to your color chart and consider the wisdom of this.

If yellow flowers are your choice, what may be included with them? First of all, as in the monochromatic, you can use all the light and dark values and the intensities of chroma. You can add the hues which are neighbors to yellow on the chart. At one side, this will include yellow-orange, orange, red-orange. On the other side, there are the yellow-greens, greens, blue-greens. In each instance, the analogy stops as it reaches the next pigment primary.

All the hues we have mentioned contain some yellow pigmentation. It is this common denominator which fixes the limits to which a yellow-based analogy may safely go. It is true that blue-green seems far removed in appearance from red-orange, but the fact remains that they can be made analogous because in both there is a trace of yellow, remote though it may seem. However, in using two such far-apart relatives, there must always be a co-ordination through intervening hues. Otherwise the effect will suggest a contrast rather than a relationship. (See Plates 6 and 16.)

Neighboring or Adjacent Hues

In developing an analogous color harmony, use neighboring or adjacent colors. First select the hue which is to be dominant. Then move progressively from one neighboring color to the next. In the yellow analogy, this suggests a gradual blending to yellow-orange, then to orange, and to red-orange, with no skips along the way. Perhaps in such an arrangement you may wish to add something from the green side, a yellow-green and spectrum green. There should be apparent that merging of closely associated hues so beautifully exemplified in the rainbow. There

must be no sense of opposition, but only a companionable projection of related and adjacent colors.

Does one always have to start with a pigment primary in
planning an analogy? Not at all. But one should stop before
entering another primary area. It is not necessary even to use a
primary color. Red-violet, violet, and blue-violet present a beautifully harmonious blend of only three hues. Blue-violet lupines,
which are rather grayed in value, combined with baptisia, which
is about the same hue but stronger in chroma, may be used with
wood violets, which are of almost spectrum intensity. Add to
these some softly grayed red-violet tulips and perhaps mauve
foxgloves, and a rich analogy is effected.

The use of a single pigment primary and its neighbors as
the limit of an analogy is not an ironclad rule. But it is one which
we do well to accept in our schedule-making and arranging and
judging. It is the limit generally imposed by decorators as they
plan interiors, and it is a well-regarded practice in the art world.

10

DIRECT COMPLEMENTS

The most obvious of all contrasting harmonies is the direct complement: a combination of any two hues which lie directly opposite on a color wheel. Red and green, blue and orange, or yellow and violet form the basic complements. However, the range extends through all the admixtures, and we find that yellow-green complements red-violet, that blue-green mates with red-orange, and blue-violet with yellow-orange.

The fact that this harmony is based upon two colors facing each other does not imply that they are politely exchanging *compliments*. The word *complement* has a more specific tale to tell; it suggests a state of completion, a fulfillment, a finality. What then, lies behind the use of such a term?

We have observed that the physical eye in perceiving a single hue also demands to see the rest of the spectrum. This phenomenon is involuntary, and usually we are unaware of it. We know now that when we stare at a red object and then close our eyes that a green object of the same form swims across the mind's eye. This is Chevreul's law of successive contrast. The missing parts of the spectrum appear as the after-image. The direct complementary harmony eliminates the need for the after-image, since the two hues presented cover the whole spectrum. Let's analyze this further.

Look at the color chart. Red and green lie opposite. Green is the composite of yellow and blue, the missing primaries. Therefore green and red are "completeness" when viewed together; they are complements. Move on to yellow and violet. Violet supplies the red and blue which, with yellow, once again adds up to the basic primaries. Blue and orange are similarly complete because orange supplies the red and yellow necessary to complement the blue.

Attraction of Contrasts

The eye-appeal of any direct complement is maintained around the color wheel, regardless of how extensive the admixture of hues. Red-orange finds its complement in blue-green; yellow-green in red-violet; yellow-orange is the opposite of blue-violet. Note further that the balance of equal primaries is always maintained. Take yellow-green and red-violet. Obviously the two primaries, yellow and red, are present, and the third, blue, is found in both the green and violet in an amount equal to each of the other two primaries. A few minutes spent in checking similar combinations around the spectrum wheel insures an understanding of contrasting harmonies. (It will also impress the spelling of the word complement!)

All this suggests again that contrasts are more immediately gratifying to the eye than related harmonies, as the monochromatic and the analogous. However, contrasts at full-spectrum intensity can prove too stimulating to be pleasant. Full attention must be paid to the use of value and chroma in any complementary har-

mony to avoid this overstimulation. Again we turn to the outdoor world for counsel. (See Plates 13 and 14.)

All contrasts produce a degree of emotional satisfaction, too.
In any pair of complements, one will come from the cool or
recessive colors; the other from the warm, advancing hues. This
creates a further sense of balance and completeness. (See Plates
8 and 10.)

Nature loves contrasting harmonies and especially the direct
complement. Consider a mile of roadside wildings. Polka dots
of blue chicory take on new sparkle where a clump of orange
day lilies grows among them. There is no competition of two
strong hues, for the blue, while unmistakable, lacks the chromatic intensity of the orange, which is at almost full-spectrum
value.

Elder in late summer offers the rich contrast of dark wine-
red berry clusters and strong yellowish-green foliage. Violet
wild iris in the marshes are pointed up by the adjacent yellow
iris. How often the violet ones are unnoticed among the tall
rushes until their complementary yellow relatives flaunt their
gold. The wood violet has a bright yellow eye to focus attention
on the less strong chroma of its petals. Nature not only shares
her spectrum generously but demonstrates the application of
color by using it in good scale, proportion, and balance. (See
Plates 7 and 9.)

The scarlet tanager has a less visible mate dressed in contrasting olive-green. Even the brown thrush seems to carry out
Nature's fancy for direct contrasts by sitting on green-blue
eggs! The cock pheasant with his green iridescent head carries
a complementary streak of scarlet on his cheek. A sugar maple,
brilliant gold against an October sky, actually is a less vibrant
contrast than first appears since the color of each leaf is somewhat muted. The seeing eye can learn from Nature's harmonies,
and the flower arranger will do well to imitate the examples
offered on every side.

The advertising business discovered early how to capitalize
on the eye-appeal of complementary harmonies. Subway posters
and magazine pages are planned to catch the attention of the

hurrying consumer and to etch a message on his memory. Intense contrasts can do this, and the flower arranger can improve her own technique through a study of advertisements.

The packaging of modern products is almost in the realm of the decorative arts. Most adroitly schemed contrasts induce us to buy by eye first and later to test, if we wish, by experience. Packaging usually employs contrasts on a rather subtle scale since a product which clamours too loud becomes strident in a well-planned interior and is subject to banishment. The next time you purchase cleaning powders or toiletries notice on the container how skillfully colors are reduced in value while still retaining the power of contrast.

Also watch your fruit-store window. See how beautifully, and possibly without any real knowledge of color, the owner places the rich purple of eggplant so as to enrich the yellow of the squashes, and how he makes the green grapes appear more luminous by grouping them near the darker red ones.

In a fruit arrangement, have you ever noticed how a touch of green or yellow leaves sets off the warm pink of peaches and the opulent purples of plums? In many of our compositions, we unwittingly rely on the eye-satisfaction of complementary hues.

A Pitfall

One pitfall awaits most arrangers when they first attempt a contrasting harmony. To a judge of any experience the story is familiar. There seems to be an irresistible temptation to effect such a color scheme by combining a container of one hue with plant material of its complement. So often the result is an exhibit which seems split in two, a competition of color which fails to qualify as anything but disharmony. I speak from long experience and my own mistakes. If blue and orange appear well combined along the roadsides why not blue flowers in an orange container or orange flowers in a blue container?

The skeleton in my container-closet is an intense blue pottery vase bought purposely for orange marigolds. It has good form, nice texture, and rich color, but somehow whenever I have used it with the planned-for marigolds, an air of ill-ease pervades the room. Even the darkest corner does not subdue the raucous impact. It took many trials to convince me that, although the colors were legitimately complementary, I was not making the best use of them. There was a quality of competitive bad manners in these two strong values which dared anyone to overlook them in the room. The blue vase, on occasion now holds soft-brown dried material with gracious acquiescence, and its color strength is more appreciated when tempered by the more delicate tonality of its complement.

The blue-and-orange marigold problem is a common one. I judge many shows in late summer, some at country fairs where the wealth of plant material makes me envious of gardeners who can produce such luxurious globes of pure chroma. I look with understanding upon the inevitable blue vase with marigolds, sometimes repeated ten or more times in a single class. Then I judge gently for I know that here are novices who need only a little time to find out their own mistakes, even as I have done.

The lesson of Christmas reds and greens cannot be passed by at this point. So often holiday tables and doorways, even trees, lose their decorative quality because there seems to be too much red and too much green in equal quantities. Red bows and bells and ornaments can overwhelm the fresh loveliness of evergreen branches. Consider the holly tree, how its mass of shiny green leaves comes to life with the twinkle of small areas of red berries. The poinsettia, on the other hand, majors in clear tropical red and subordinates its green complement. There is a place for both dominants, red and green, and this can be true of any combination, one hue for the prima donna, the other for the supporting cast, according to the needs of the arranger. (See Plates 13 and 14.)

In spring, the apple tree raises a parasol of blossoms, delicately pink, when there are few leaves to set up a green contrast. In late summer the lush green foliage is able to support the glowing mass of red apples along its boughs. This is a suggestion on how to use different values of the same pair of complements.

44

SPLIT COMPLEMENTS

In the split complement occurs a gracious variation of the direct complement. Now three colors are combined. Starting with a hue and moving toward its opposite, we bypass it, and instead select the colors on either side. The red and green of the direct contrast is replaced by red with blue-green and yellow-green. Or starting with green, the split complement allows the inclusion of red-violet and red-orange. A rather subtle example is found in Lilium speciosum rubrum, the "rubrum lily" of many gardens. Springing from green stalk and leaves, the trumpet of faintly tinted white is freckled strongly with red-violet while the furry anthers hold masses of red-orange pollen. (Incidentally, while you may wish to protect yourself against the clinging habits of this pollen, please do not remove the anthers and so deprive this handsome bloom of a distinctive color effect.)

A stalk of hybrid delphinium may be dominantly violet-blue but an occasional red-violet floret and the yellow centers provide a definite split complementary harmony. Many of the iris and the hybrid tea roses on examination show this same split personality. The fact that we so often must search for this harmony in a flower offers a lesson. The secret of a successful contrast of this kind depends upon letting one hue be dominant and the other two subordinate, and usually each in a varying degree of importance. Once again Nature is the student's guide. (See Plate 12.)

In classifying flowers which exemplify split complements, I have been amazed that the one most commonly found is also the one we feel is so difficult to endure—the red-orange, red-violet combination. How we shudder at the flower border which includes both magenta and red-orange zinnias and vow never again to plant a packet of mixed seeds. Yet when the identical combination occurs on a flower, it is so skillfully blended that we actually enjoy the softly modulated dissonances.

Double Split Complement

This is a variation of the foregoing harmony with the hues on either side of both direct complements combined, thus giving six colors with which to work. A double split complementary harmony stemming from an orange and blue contrast will offer blue, red-orange, and yellow-orange combined with orange, blue-green, and blue-violet. This latitude provides a more flexible use of plant materials. However, the untrained eye may find that a suitable blending of six hues can prove as unmanageable as driving three teams of horses. This never should deter us from having the fun of trying out such a scheme. Mistakes may be glaring enough to indicate just where keener judgment should be exercised for better results.

The individual character of most flowers makes it difficult to find specimens which illustrate the double split harmony. It appears in well-planned gardens, in textiles and wallpapers where the possibilities have been explored by experts whose trained vision develops solutions which the less skillful can exploit. I have found that some Rex begonia leaves while appearing to hold two colors, almost fall into the classification of double split complements. The basic leaf hue is green, dark blue-green with yellow-green markings; the stems have hairs and splotches of red, red-violet, and red-orange of dark value. This example strains a little to make its point but from such a close harmony as appears in these leaves may come a suggestion for a more elaborate composition.

Beneath my window at this moment, a massed planting of "blue" hydrangeas forms a background for hybrid hemerocallis ranging from yellow through red-orange. Color samples in hand, I have just tried to determine what color harmony they represent. From a quick glance, it appears to be a direct complement but the color chart shows an amazing range of hues. Actually there are no truly blue flowers there. Green-blue, blue-violet, and red-violet are found among the hydrangea florets. Hemerocallis provide the contrasts which set up the following split complementary harmonies; green-blue and violet-blue with orange. There is also blue-violet and red-violet with yellow. No wonder the hydrangeas and day lilies are so exquisite against the white house. Their sharp contrast is made more tolerable by a nearby group of blue-green junipers so softly grayed that they modify the chroma of the flowers. (See Plate 16.)

Read over the colors mentioned in this last paragraph. You will notice something which is apparently a discrepancy. I have spoken of green-blue and blue-green. This brings out an important point. Earlier it was pointed out that in describing a tertiary color the primary hue was mentioned first, the secondary next, as blue-green. That means an equal mixture. However, the color *green-blue* shows that there is a preponderance of blue and a lesser amount of green. This is brought up here, rather than earlier, that you may compare the distinction in terminology as shown in a specific example.

Let us now return to the flowers themselves. When I bring a handful of them into the house, however, I have to make a choice. Their contrast is so dominant that, arranged, they must either be placed near an open window where sunlight tempers their intensity, or allowed to overpower other objects in the room. An old copper container with reddish overlay brings soft-voiced persuasion to their brashness and a gray-blue wall further tempers the day-lily dynamics, though both container and wall are a repetitive contrast.

12

TRIADS

From the neighborly congeniality of related harmonies and the forceful contrasts of complements, we now approach a combination which seems to lead back to the start, and to the entire spectrum. The triad actually carries the eye not only across the wheel but all around it. Should an equilateral triangle be placed on a color chart, its three angles would touch three equidistant hues. Starting with yellow, we immediately perceive that the other two primaries of blue and red complete the triangle. Or with green as the first angle, the other secondaries of orange and violet form the triad, and so on.

The completeness of this harmony is too evident to need further explanation. At first it might seem that a harmony composed of three such divergent hues would fail to achieve balance. Actually, the triad is used as frequently as any other contrast and happens to be an extremely popular one for interiors. Think of how many pleasant rooms you know which prove this. Gray-blue walls with golden yellow hangings are more interesting if a sofa or pair of chairs adds a warm red accent. A bedroom with soft peach walls and a mossy green rug gains interest when a third color is introduced in chintz or linen printed with light and dark values of violet; those we call orchid, wisteria, or eggplant, with spectrum violet to complete the triad.

Military uniforms throughout the centuries have shown a preference for blue with gallant gold braid and buttons and a scarlet cockaded hat. Gothic stained glass featured the triad of primaries, and oriental rugs glow with the same combination.

Completeness of Triads

Artists have always found that this harmony provides a sense of fulfillment and completeness. The Italian primitives show it in bright clear values very close to spectrum chroma. Painted chests of the Dutch settlers in our own land reflect the same taste. Giotto and Fra Angelico, each in his way seemed to prefer the unity of the full triadic range of the color spectrum. Giotto's work appears subdued, due, perhaps, to the medium he employed. Fra Angelico painted with such ephemeral lightness that every angel feather seemed to be of purest gold dust. Raphael not only used the design of the triangle but echoed it in the triadic red, yellow, and blue. Perhaps none of these artists is scrupulously faithful to a spectrum triad but these examples assure us that such a harmony is rewarding to try. (See Plate 2.)

At harvest time, roadside stands show preference for triadic schemes. Orange pumpkins and squash, the deep purple of eggplant and cabbage and plums find a third companion in the greens of late spinach, broccoli, and kale. A small sample of a springtime triad lies within the flower of a violet crocus. Stoop to examine it crouched in the early green of grass, and notice that the usual yellow stamens are in this instance true spectrum orange, completing a miniature triadic scheme.

Many of you have already reached for your color charts to

test the truth of all this. I hope so, for this will open a way for new and fresh explorations into the harmonic chords which Nature is using continually. It is so easy to be content with combinations of colors which have long pleased the eye, and to shrug off the suggestions for new and startling possibilities. It becomes art when the untried evolves into something exciting enough to bring forth praise from the beholder. And let's never forget the judge who is always eager to recognize that elusive quality, distinction.

From triads we might move on to tetrads, the use of four equidistant hues, but the triads already discussed offer a territory wide enough for any arranger in search of adventure.

13

SYMBOLISM AND ASSOCIATION

The emotional response to the spectrum and its blended harmonies is almost as involuntary as the physical fact of vision.
It results in a personal appraisal of something which becomes
either pleasurable or distasteful, but it also stems from an instinc-
tive association between hues and ideas. We have already re-
marked on the sense of pride we feel as the red, white, and blue
of the American flag passes in parade. Behind this combination
of colors there is a tradition; the flag is a symbol. The red represents the courage which has made our country great; the white,
freedom and purity of purpose; and the blue, the loyalty we owe
it. Without the symbolism of color the flag would have less
meaning for us. Its color associations are important; they are
a kind of code by which we express our own emotions and
interpret sympathetically the emotional expression of others.

Symbolism lies in the realm of classic expression. It belongs to the ages. It is a summing-up of age-long experiences. We who work with color should use this symbolism respectfully. The so-called "patriotic arrangement" called for at flower shows is often ludicrous despite its sincere motivation. I have seen this class interpreted by striped groupings of red, white, and blue flowers without design or imagery. The worst offender is the flag replica, in which red and white flowers are laid in a rectangle like an old-time funerary "pillow" with the "stars" shining against a purple—not a blue—field. This appears too frequently to pass unchallenged.

It is possible with flowers to express patriotic ideals or to celebrate a national event without such realism—and particularly with a hue which is not even accurate. For some years, I was invited to judge a show which repeated its annual errors in spite of the conscientious criticisms of the judges. Each time, we gently pointed out the difference between blue and violet; each time in came the purported patriotism. It got to be a game among the judges to count the repetitions, yet we were concerned enough to bear down on the culprits year after year. We lost out and were not invited back after the fifth year. We heard that our decisions were considered too exacting by the "patriots." For us it had ceased to be amusing, only frustrating.

What Is a Symbol?

What do we mean by the symbolism of color? The word symbol comes from Greek, and means a token, an emblem, something that stands for something else. It is like a single coin which is equal in value to a number of smaller coins, rich in its simplification of several values into one. It is not necessary to indicate realistically what is told symbolically. We should use color symbolism with imagination and expect to be understood through the beholder's knowledge of the token. The government does not verbally praise each brave soldier for his particular act of heroism; he is given a medal, a *token* of appreciation. When he wears it, all who see, read his story at a glance.

To return to the patriotic harmony, a *replica* of the flag is far less stirring than the original, certainly a misguided use of plant material. But I have been moved by a starlike arrangement of white carnations against a flag-blue textile; the luminous quality of the flowers conveyed a spiritual meaning. I also recall a composition of red gladiolus poised like outspread wings on a group of slate-blue rocks—the American eagle on a crag! These imaginative pieces evoked more response from judges and public than a contrived flag could possibly have done.

When we rely upon symbolism to make the most of color, we must be aware of the traditional story which belongs to each hue. This will not be the same in the West, say, as in the Far East. If a class calls for a composition interpretive of a particular country, some research may be required into color symbolism. We may rely on an accepted color code for our part of the globe. In this reference, red may include red-orange and violet-red; yellow, yellow-orange, and yellow-green, and so on. Remember that a symbol is but a token and never tells anything but an imaginary tale.

For Red

Nature gives us red in fire. Since fire was one of primitive man's few assets, he became acutely conscious of its color, and looked for red in other sources. The animals he killed for food were obtained at the risk of life; therefore blood-red meant sacrifice and danger. The early church adopted red as the color of martyrdom. Today it bespeaks the blood of heroes, the "red badge of courage."

Red also is a symbol of love, and the red rose was a lady's token to her knight. Conversely, evil is identified with a red devil in tights and tail. Intense red, therefore, no matter what the emotion, love or hate, is a dynamic color. (See Plates 9 and 10.)

Lighter values of red have a different significance; they are feminine. Pink and soft rosy hues were the favorites of many French painters catering to court tastes during royalist days.

Rose color was the favorite of Madame de Pompadour, mistress of Louis XV. When she started the porcelain works at Sèvres, the pink rose was featured on early pieces. Watteau and Greuze, painting at the same time, used the delectable "pompadour pinks."

Darker values of red are identified with the sombre canvases of Spanish painters. Velásquez and Goya loved their rich qualities, as did the masters of the Italian Renaissance.

For Orange

The vibrancy of orange is associated with the sun and its vitalizing warmth. There is a radiance in orange. It is a dramatic color useful for sharp effect, and almost too dazzling except in controlled amounts. Look at an advertisement for oranges or frozen orange juice. See how the color of the fruit lends eye-appeal to the message. It actually seems to radiate nourishing vitamins. In Nature, orange appears in marigolds and zinnias, in butterfly weed and calendulas and umbellatum lilies which talk back with good temper to the hot sun himself. On bitter winter mornings the great orange ball of the rising sun shining on icy trees has an encouraging look of warmth.

Byzantine art makes frequent use of the golden radiance of orange and its admixtures. Its chroma symbolizes an opulence dear to the East. Persian miniatures relied on the lighter, yet strong, chromatic charms of this hue, with melon and apricot and peach to suggest the color of fruits native to the country's gardens. There is a clarity in these values which tempers the power of spectrum orange to a more delicate effect.

In the dark and grayed values of orange, browns assert themselves. For us, brown is autumnal; it suggests waning vigor, and the reluctant passing of the colors of summer. But browns can be warm and rich, too, belying the suggestion of a "dark brown taste" and the dull muddy-brown interiors of the early twentieth century.

As a gardener jealous of my compost heap, I rage when I see brown leaves set on fire in the fall. However, a sense of color compensation assuages my anger as I see the brown, dead-looking leaves break up into flames of yellow and red, so symbolic of the orange which they comprise. As the smoke ascends it seems like a pagan supplication to the sun-god for a more benevolent winter ahead.

For Yellow

Yellow is a most versatile hue, conspicuous in harmonies throughout the history of art. It is the color we see as light coming in soft gleams from the sun, from electric lamps, and in candlelight. It is an inspiring hue, full of promise, and of symbolism. It signifies the gold of an emperor; in ancient China yellow was reserved for royalty. Napoleon chose "golden bees" as token of his successful empire-building, and as a symbol for Bonaparte. Fairy-tale princesses always ride in golden coaches, as did a modern queen to her coronation. Yellow is a hue so filled with the goodness of all things that Nature seems to have introduced it in every possible way. It is the common color of velvet pollen, and it appears in every landscape. It is present in the green of grass, and in the cups of many blossoms. (See Plate 3.)

Artists delight in the sunlit values of yellow. Vermeer in particular has used it adroitly to suggest sun-touched areas. Rembrandt lighted with yellow his superbly characterized faces emerging from the shadows.

In arrangements, when in doubt, introduce a bit of yellow. I have found it adds spirit when a little lift is needed, and it inclines to unite inharmonious companions. Flower faces would often look dull were it not for their bright yellow eyes.

It is difficult to reconcile this lovely color with the "yellow streak" of cowardice or to understand why the flag of pestilence is yellow. There is also, of course, the symbolism of unlovely things, but in the flower world, yellow happily typifies springtime and gaiety.

For Green

This is Nature's own color as no one dares deny. It is associated with vigor and hopefulness and the reappearance of life in early spring, so it signifies eternity and immortality. Green laurel and bay, woven into wreaths for the winners in the Greek and Roman games, now symbolize victory. It is associated with dryads and the youthful characters of mythology. Indeed, green typifies young naïveté, but it also is the symbol of "green-eyed jealousy."

In art, tapestries make full use of all values of green as backgrounds for trees and floral designs. It is a color associated with cool shade and deep forests, and so has a restful meaning. As in Nature, green can always be used as a foil for other hues. (See Plate 15.)

For Blue

"True-blue" typifies steadfastness and loyalty. Possibly the vast reaches of sea and sky which seemed to define the limits of the early universe made people associate the color with immutability. The word blue does not appear often in ancient records, and possibly it was a color not found in many natural forms. It is a cold color, and in its darker values lacks the appeal of warmer hues. Its suggestion of stability never wavers, however.

The most popular blues—and blue is a favorite—are found in mixtures tending toward violet. These gain warmth through even a minimum of red. The classic blue which we associate with French painters and Wedgwood ceramics is a heritage from ancient Greece. The pure clear blue called the Virgin's color and used by the old masters for Our Lady's robe, keeps its ecclesiastical connotation today. The association of blue with the cool depths of water (an illusion, since water is colorless) gives it a sense of quietude and repose.

Nature offers few true blues; many flowers so designated in catalogues really are tinged with violet. The forget-me-not, anchusa, delphinium, cornflower are faithful to the primary hue. Blue spruces and blue junipers are really grayed blue-green. (See Plates 11 and 12.)

For Violet

There seems to be a mystic beauty in this most recessive of hues, which probably explains its association with penitence and mourning. Yet it is a hue which has served royalty on its great occasions and is used by church dignitaries. From red, violet gets a modicum of warmth and spirit, but its blue content emphasizes its secretive withdrawal. In Nature, the violet range is generous; there are many wildflowers as well as cultivated plants. The regal dignity of violet combines well with almost all harmonies. (See Plate 2.)

Beyond traditional usage, colors often develop personal associations. The color of the dress worn for a wonderful dance may become a favorite, but the color of the suit we had on in an accident may never return to favor. The color of flowers which arrive *after* an operation may always have a pleasant association. So it is that the mind collects a multitude of color symbols which continue to add meaning to the eye's perception.

14

COLOR AND THE PRINCIPLES
OF DESIGN

The flower arranger may have misgivings at this point. On one hand, there are theories and laws governing color; on the other, the fact that color in plant materials does not always adapt itself to theories and laws. Actually there is no need to reconcile the two points. Color is a natural phenomenon, exempt from manmade laws. What science has done is to organize the subject of color so that we can use it effectively. In our work with plants, science should be our guide but not our master.

If there is no truly monochromatic piece of plant material, then it is not possible to produce a plant harmony without a trace of another color—and we should not try. It is enough if we select leaves and flowers of one hue and consider inconsequential the incidence of leaf-veins or pollen in another color. (See Plate 5.)

This flexibility applies to all interpretations of the rules relating to fixed pigments. Plate 8 shows a direct complementary scheme, but the poppies have centers of dark blue, a third color. However, the spirit of this arrangement would have been lost if another flower had been substituted. The blue-green cedrus and the red-orange blooms were the best that could be found to illustrate this harmony, and also show contrast of texture and form.

The choice was deliberate; the plants were at their colorful best at the same time, and the container was too weighty to accept a less imposing flower form. You may notice, though, that the heads of several of the poppies were turned so that there would be a minimum intrusion of the third hue. Only those needed to unify the design were permitted to look out with wide-open splendor. All this illustrates the essential fact that color should be considered only after the principles of design have been applied; also that color is never independent of the elements of line and form and texture.

Color in Design

How, then, does one apply color to design? Suppose the impulse which lies behind an arrangement has been inspired by a burst of chroma in the garden or suggested by some soft blending in muted hues in Nature. Can design start from a color stimulus if color is always subordinate to design?

Have you ever seen a room decorated around a painting or piece of sculpture or a fine Aubusson rug? Given some treasure as an inspiration, the next step is to design a place where it can be displayed. Beautiful as any individual item or color may be, it loses much of its charm if it is not wisely placed. A sculpture jostled by mediocre ceramics or a painting dimmed by blatant draperies is less beautiful. Carelessly used, color is meaningless even when applied to a well-balanced and well-proportioned pattern. Superbly chosen, color is ineffective in a poor design. This is not the place to go into the subject of design at length but it is not possible to bypass the principles in any discussion pertinent to a form of artistic expression.

What Is Design?

According to the dictionary design is "an arrangement of forms and color or both, intended to be wrought out for ornament, a pattern, a co-ordination of materials." When we wish to create a design, there must be an organized plan to guide us. The plan need not be complex. For most of us each day has its design—rise, bathe, dress, eat, work, relax, retire. That is the structure of an average day. The colorful incidents, the joys and sorrows, are forms contained within this pattern.

A house is designed. It has floors, wall, and roof, bare essentials in structure but without them ornaments have little value. So it is with flower arrangement. There must be a structure which is usually based upon a skeleton of lines, either straight or curved. This linear pattern may be strengthened by the addition of forms—leaf or flower or bud. There should be variation in the forms as oval, round, spike, or sphere. The co-ordination of line and form is best accomplished when accepted principles of art are followed. Color and texture are but additional ornament. These four together comprise the elements of design; they are building materials.

The proper assembling of the building materials or elements is important. For this, there is an old blueprint, a set of rules or principles which have been used for so many centuries that they represent the classic procedure for the architect, the artist, the sculptor, the weaver, and also the flower arranger. Let us review these principles, each of which is dependent upon all the others for a successful result.

Proportion

Proportion involves the correct use of space. Design begins with a problem of space; it cannot be overlooked. A mass planting of tall evergreens in front of a modest house is not properly related to space. Tall sunflowers are out of proportion in a narrow perennial border. Within a given area objects should be comfortably composed without seeming to jostle or crowd. Nor should they appear inadequate and lost.

Color must be applied proportionately also. A mass of intense color will emerge far larger than a similar area of less vivid hues. The recessive quality of green foliage provides an excellent foil for a small amount of brighter chroma. A dark mass in a light container will be less appealing than one which includes a good proportion of light and medium and dark. The cool colors are never proportionately assertive as are the warmer hues. Nature teaches this, too.

The luna moth on Plate 13. is a masterpiece of design in structure, and its colors are deployed in the same masterly fashion. While the moth is generally light in its color values, delicate and fragile, there is also an introduction of a dark color, so restrained that there is no apparent weightiness. The darker hue is applied in such superb proportion that it serves as an accent only. In the floral interpretation of this example, Plate 14., I tried to keep the color in approximately the same proportion of light to dark, of value to value.

Scale

Scale involves the relationship of sizes in parts of a composition, each form to its neighbor. One petunia in a ten-inch container is out of scale. A cluster of petunias, with buds and half-developed blooms and fully opened flowers arranged with a compatible leaf form would be a step toward solving the problem of scale. A stalk of iris combined with a peony is not only poor use of line and form but there is no kinship in the sizes.

Scale is closely allied to proportion; unless the units brought together in a design are in proper scale, there is no chance that the final proportion will be pleasing. Color is used in good scale if there is a gradation not only of the size of the blooms but also in the relative intensity of each hue. In Plate 2. it has been possible to combine six hues because the color was applied with consideration for the size of each form and its place in the whole mass. The most dominant triad employs forms and colors of relatively equal chroma. The triad which is less important is stated in colors of lesser chroma and value. Notice that there is a graded scale of color notes throughout the composition.

The scale of containers is most important. A strong-hued vase holding weak little items suggests the frightened children in the fiery furnace. A small, neutral-colored vase holding a great dahlia or oversized leaves appears to be bursting its seams.

Balance

Good balance brings stability and security to a design. In flower arrangement, balance is not a matter of actual weight as when a five-pound box of sugar on one side of a scale balances the small iron weight on the other side.

There is a visual balance, an illusion we might say. A large mass of intensely colored or dark-hued blooms in a small container will appear topheavy and insecure. This is not always due to the relative scale or proportion of the flower mass to its container. Such instability often stems from the choice of material whose color appears too strong or too heavy in value to balance the lighter area of the container. The vase may be a piece of pottery actually weighing several ounces more than the flowers themselves, yet visually, the color—and perhaps the form—of the arrangement destroys its balanced stability.

Color is an effective way of achieving balance. Generally paler hues and lighter values have a delicacy, an airiness which makes them useful on the edges of an arrangement. Darker hues and lower values have greater visual weight; they focus attention where equilibrium must be sustained. A bright color topping a soft-toned arrangement seems to pull it over on its face. That same bright intensity near the focal point becomes an effective control. An experienced artist may be able to evade this general rule successfully but only because she is skilled enough to do it without violating the major principle of balance.

Balance of color is best attained with unequal amounts. A spot of spectrum green will never equal a similar spot of spectrum red because each has a different impact of chroma. (See Plates 9. and 10.) A spot of red against a larger mass of green will appear satisfying. The discerning eye selects a larger amount of one hue or value and creates a feeling of ease and stability by using with it a smaller area of potent chroma or value. Plate 16. shows how adequately a slight spot of bright yellow sustains balance against a proportionately large area of muted blue-green.

Rhythm

Rhythm adds interest to any composition because it is a device which lures the eye of the beholder to see everything in a picture yet controls the movement so skillfully that the eye is forced to return to the most important feature. There are two kinds of rhythm, one achieved by a repetition of line, form, or color so that there is a steady emphasis on a single element. The other rhythm is more lyric, flowing like a melody which moves along yet still follows a studied pattern and never loses control. (See Plates 10., 12., and 14.)

Nature displays both types; one in a range of mountain peaks in majestic march, each gaining importance because it is part of a succession of similar forms. That is architectural rhythm. The other rhythm, like a river, flows along in pleasant curves and with beguiling perspectives, controlled by the banks on either side yet attracting the eye along all its meanderings.

The flower arranger can easily achieve rhythm with the lovely lines of living plants, and color is a strong ally. The linear pattern sets the theme and various forms enhance it, but color makes it move and vibrate so that a composition comes alive. Bright hues more obviously maintain the rhythmic line but the position of even the most muted ones can, by quiet insistence, demand attention. It is through repetition of color that rhythm is best attained.

The color plates in Part Three show ways in which color carries out the rhythm of the design either through repetitive use of a hue or by stopping the eye at a crucial spot and interrupting the motion by introducing another color to make a point of emphasis. We must always be careful, however, to make such color changes only a pause and let the color rhythm then move on to carry the eye further. It is through rhythm that good balance often results, a motion which encompasses all yet provides a feeling of finality at the visual center of a composition.

Dominance and Contrast

Dominance and contrast react upon each other. In any design one part must be more important than another. A newspaper account carries a banner headline; subheads emphasize the same news. A contrast is established which stresses the relative importance of the facts of the story. A group of magenta phlox creeping into a well-disciplined garden may dominate to a point of irritation. A group of yellow lady slippers in the deep reaches of a hemlock grove is a dominant note made stronger by contrast with surrounding plants. (See Plates 5. and 6.)

Color is emphatic in any design; it must be used with an awareness of how prominently a spot of bright chroma seems to dominate an area of lesser values. But contrast of very light values and very dark values lacks character, and both become neutralized and uninteresting. So often a flower-show schedule calls for a monochrome based upon red and the exhibitor chooses to combine dark red roses with light pink stock or snapdragons. It is a safe monochrome but lacks any distinction. This is because the tint is relatively as light as the shade is dark; neither is dominant and there is no decisive contrast. Sometimes a rich, lustrous clump of coleus leaves will add the missing values and so stimulate the whole color scheme. The blue vase and orange marigolds mentioned elsewhere in this book is an example of two strong hues which fail to succeed because neither dominates while the other acts as a support.

Sometimes an exotic flower, unfamiliar or rare, assumes too important a place in an arrangement. For many years there was a prejudice against orchids in arrangements. Judges were advised to look upon these lovely flowers with a disdain due the nouveau riche. What lay behind this practice was not any offense on the part of the poor orchid. An unimaginative exhibitor had used a choice specimen—and an expensive one—without relevance to other factors. The result was like a little girl dressed up in her mother's jewels; the orchid was too dominant for good taste.

The prohibition against orchids and their rare companions stemmed from a snobbish evaluation and had nothing to do with their contribution to design. Now that exotic and new plants are more available to us, arrangers tend to capitalize the dominant form or color of unusual specimens. This is fine. Without their imaginative use we might soon lose these imports. However, their exotic coloring and forms must be related to the basic pattern. The unique can be misleading. If dominance leads to a finer exhibit, that is art; if it leads to something bizarre and tasteless, it violates the underlying principles of true beauty.

15

KINSHIP OF COLOR AND TEXTURE

Since color is a sensation produced by light rays striking an object, it follows that the character of a surface will affect the ultimate color we see. Glossy, hard finishes throw back the light and produce the bright patches we call high lights. A rough surface with its tiny hills and valleys of uneven penetration grays all colors. A sleek chintz and a piled rug may be dyed in the same mixture yet the colors will look different because of textural variations. Irregularity in the form of an object has the same effect.

In the plant kingdom, there is a vast range of textures. The smooth silk of the tuberous begonia blossom differs from the crinkled silk of a petunia. The organdy-like crispness of carnations is not the same as the shaggy wool of some chrysanthemums. The depth of texture in dahlias is due to the curving of each petal as it is caught at the calyx; their velvet look is produced by shadows on the diminishing depth. Actually, the fastened end of the petal may be lighter although it appears darker in the mass. Thus texture influences color perception.

Trees are often identified by the textural differences in their bark. Evergreens of similar chroma appear dissimilar because light is reflected variably on their textured, massed needles. Even with its own loveliness, color gains immeasurably because of the added charm of texture. (See Plates 4., 13., and 14.)

Relationship of textures is important to color harmonies. Contrast of textures is only interesting when the elements balance. Nature uses textural opposites in many ways. The rough, prickly stem and coarse leaves of a thistle are in contrast to the delicate flower filaments. However, a mass of these filaments combined in the large flower head provides adequate balance of textures. This contradiction of coarse and fine, well integrated, in a single plant, makes thistles one of our most dramatic wildings, despite their usurpation of pastureland.

Other specimens maintain a similarity; tulip smooth and sleek throughout; ageratum woolly and rough. Queen Anne's lace is aptly named, with leaves and blooms equally lacy. Because of their broken texture the near-white flowers appear shadowy gray.

Relation of Containers

The container may be a contrast or a repetition of the floral textures. Proper selection of container is something every arranger must learn for herself. Once we all struggled under the stupid rule that roses must be used only in silver or fine crystal. The reason behind this was probably related to a supposed need for similar qualities of textures. Such rules are too inflexible; there are many kinds of roses both elegant and rugged. Some species roses never look well in crystal; pottery is right for them. Rules should never be limiting. We must learn to appreciate distinctions in quality. These alone give a sound perspective for successful combinations.

Compatibility of textures has nothing to do with cost or rarity. Maidenhair fern, ethereal in substance, grows happily along wooded roadsides with coarser weeds. Its constant companion is Christmas fern, strong and sturdy; yet each complements, not imitates, the other.

Maidenhair fern looks well in fragile glass suited to its apparent weightlessness. Gardenias and metals seem not remotely akin, yet fine pewter reflects their textural smoothness. Rose of Sharon grows with democratic unconcern for its neighbors, yet its blossoms rival the quality of old Chinese porcelain.

When lecturing, I show textiles with flower arrangements. The audience instinctively rejects combinations which are not good. Often I ask them to analyze the color relationship of flowers, containers, and fabrics. The choice of material seems agreeable enough yet the composition lacks harmony. I substitute another textile of similar hue but of more compatible texture, and the applause is spontaneous. This proves that often what we misjudge as a color fault actually is an inconsistency in textures. The fact that pigments are surface colors should make us aware of the influence of texture upon color perception. (See Plates 15. and 16.)

3

Color: Where We Find It

COLOR PLATES

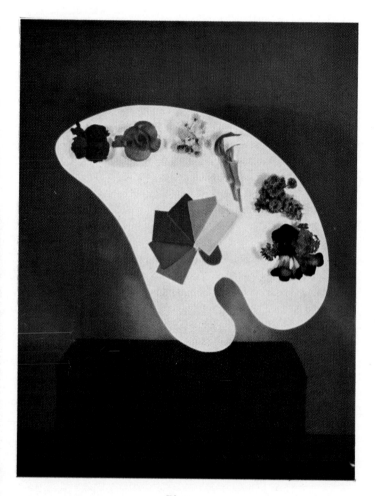

Plate 1.

Plate 2.

Plate 3.

Plate 4.

Plate 5.

Plate 6.

Plate 7.

Plate 8.

Plate 9.

Plate 10.

Plate 11.

Plate 12.

Plate 13.

Plate 14.

Plate 15.

Plate 16.

I hope you agree that color is not to be measured mathematically, at least by the arranger, and that the few manmade rules which govern it are to be interpreted with a flexibility matching Nature's untrammeled use of color. On every side a great text book lies open for us to study earth's own lessons of color.

The pictures which follow show color as we find it in natural forms—on a moth's wing or a bird's feather; in the gleam of a mineral or the brightness of a woodland flower; on lichened stump, and in the world beneath the sea. Each natural element has been interpreted in an arrangement using familiar materials but in a less familiar way. Each picture tells a story of a color harmony, not rigidly obedient to rules but still conforming to good usage.

With seeking eye, you will find other hues in natural specimens, and with creative ingenuity, you will produce many lovely arrangements of your own. You, too, will have the fun of discovering color all about you and making it into a pattern with your own hands, as I have done. If these pictures appear to take liberties with color, I assure you that each problem has been checked for fidelity to the color chart. This is not my usual method. I prefer to be free from restrictions which sacrifice either design or ideal to obedience to rules, but this is a study book and real effort has been made to stress specific points.

Actually color is a freely-given gift, found everywhere. You should use it freely.

COLOR HARMONIES FROM
NATURE WITH INTERPRETIVE
FLOWER ARRANGEMENTS

Plate 1. The Gardener's Palette

Only the shape of this classic palette belongs to the painter from whom it was borrowed to show the flower arranger's working colors. The flowers were selected, color chart in hand, to match the spectrum hues as accurately as natural and synthetic pigments ever permit. Except for red, faithful color examples were surprisingly easy to find in my late spring garden and among my house plants.

Red carnations, orange tuberous begonias, yellow Dutch iris and daisies, green Jack-in-the-pulpit, blue cornflowers and delphinium, violet gloxinias, lupines, and annual phlox are all true in color. Only the green lacks full spectrum intensity. It is amazing that in all the wealth of green, which might be considered the most available hue, there is almost no example of true spectrum chroma. Certainly nothing in the average garden fills this need, and I believe that only an occasional tropical plant approximates it. The Jack had the greatest fidelity to true green.

The color cards clasping the palette at the thumb hole are placed in reverse, each pointing to its direct complement.

The white palette is a symbol of the source of all color—white light; and a reminder that white is a pigment, not a spectrum color. The palette is posed on black velvet to simulate the absence of light and to include black also as a pigment. The grayed background represents the third neutral in the trio.

Plate 2.   Capturing the Complete Spectrum

To attempt to integrate all spectrum hues in a single arrangement is dangerous. There is no law to govern such harmony, but, having assembled samples for the palette, I was challenged to collect from the garden, flowers of the same colors and to put them together. I used two sets of triads, one based on primary colors and one on the secondaries.

The blue delphinium, the red and the yellow roses were of strongest color and form and so composed the dominant triad. The secondaries had to be subordinate in form, in value, and in chroma. The only large unit among these was the violet iris. Because of low chroma and large form, this helped balance the smaller yellow iris and so contributed to a vertical stability.

Smaller amounts of the primaries were used to give variety of form and also transition in scale—yellow daisies and snapdragons and curving lupine, lighter in value than the delphinium. Orange only appears in the very delicate peach stock which co-ordinates all parts of the arrangement.

Contradicting a belief that light values do not have enough visual weight for a center of interest, the cluster of peach stock actually stabilizes the whole with a bright gleam among the dark roses. To relate the mass arrangement to the tall container, yellow-green fruits of andromeda and red-violet fuchsias, combining the colors in both triads, were selected to complete the design.

The neutral values of the creamy alabaster container and black marble table reflect the textural fineness of the flowers. The background is dark gray-green of very low value.

Plate 3. Color on the Wing

In the neutral austerity of winter outdoors, we become more aware of bird coloration as the population of our feeding station grows. Camouflage experts have always turned to birds and small animals to perfect their techniques; we who would achieve finer harmonies with flowers might follow their lead. If the colors of a bird blend well enough to afford concealment, then they should be good examples of unity and harmony for us to copy. We soon discover that feathers are not always colored with pigment but often owe their hues to the refraction of surface light.

The meadowlark shown here is, amazingly, a monochromatic bird. I checked with color samples in hand and found that his yellow breast color appears on wings and back in lower values of beige and brown. The yellow is intensified by the black bib, a lesson in contrast. A bird of country meadows, the lark nests among dried leaves and grasses which repeat the tweedlike coloration which conceals him well. The breast color matches the marsh marigolds, yellow iris, buttercups, and goldenrod which bloom nearby in their seasons.

Bird colors often suggest types of arrangements. The meadowlark might be described by grasses, leaves, and black-eyed Susans in a basket, or as shown here. The oriole with his sleek black seems to represent country-house sophistication, and the tanager might represent the gay migrant folk who frequent expensive resorts.

Plate 4. Meadowlark Gold—a Monochromatic Harmony

The meadowlark's true monochrome was difficult to translate into a flower arrangement. Actually his color is not primary yellow but yellow with a trace of orange; the hue is really yellow orange-yellow. This admixture is found on a large chart between yellow and yellow-orange—a very fine distinction but a discernible one. It was imperative to have all plant materials and container faithful to one color to achieve a monochromatic harmony.

I chose the semicactus dahlias for their feathery petals and their petal-tips touched with a faintly darker value. Prince's-feather matched in color but added a new line and texture. The leaves of Kalanchoe beharensis added a sculptured form and darker values of rich yellow-brown velvet.

For a container, I first considered a maple mortar of good color and texture but the form proved bulky. Next came tôle, rejected as too elegant in style and of unsuitable texture; then pottery, too coarse; copper, no distinction. Finally I chose the "duck." He was born in a wood lot and with slight human touching-up bred into this amusing piece of modern "sculpture." His color and texture were excellent, but the linear pattern could not be broken at any point. Therefore the arrangement was planned to stand behind, imitating his stance, yet with an identity of its own. The kalanchoe leaves, a transition that follows the curves of neck and tail, complete the composition.

Plate 5.   Nature's Various Analogies

Each season presents a new set of analogous colors. Spring opens the year with yellow daffodils, yellow-green willow wands, and the pure green of newborn grass. Summer is more generous, including the entire spectrum in flowers and fruits. The colors of pink zinnias and phlox, violet-red cockscomb, buddleia in royal purple, and violet platycodon are repeated in pink-cheeked peaches, violet-red cabbage, and the blue-violet of Concord grapes. Winter is less colorful but there is yellow-green arborvitae, deep green hemlock, holly, and rhododendron, and blue-green spruces for an analogy.

Autumn compensates for winter's frugality with a generous array of leaf forms and colors.

In this contrived bouquet each leaf-design offers a lesson. One "flower" is yellow-green, yellow, and orange. Another combines yellow and yellow-orange with orange accent. The largest shows orange, red-orange, red, and red-violet with the flower-center straying into the forbidden yellow primary, but only as a bow to the vagaries of the bloom.

In a mass on trees, all these hues appear more intense, evidence of the power of a quantity of color and its relation to the extent of an area. Individually the leaves are muted like the echo of a song that is sung. The three oak leaves with the red-orange pyracantha form an almost monochromatic trio. There are other autumn analogies to which we may go for different harmonies of related hues.

Plate 6. Contrast of Values

In the two related applications of autumn analogies, foliage and fruits, both dried and fresh, appear in a wall piece, which recalls once-vibrant intensities, and in a table piece where succulent fruit flaunts them boldly. The background of yellow-green like sunlight is repeated in artichokes opened to show their own lovely analogy of pale yellow, yellow-green, and grayed green, with tips of darkened yellow. Here, in a single fruit, is a complete color scheme.

Leaves of Magnolia grandiflora and grapes co-ordinate all the hues. Bland yellow apples, large in form but not weighty in value are balanced by the strong chroma but small forms of kumquats. Large shiny persimmons are partially concealed to modify their vivid red-orange. Bosc pears in browns, derived from both yellow and orange, lower the tonality to the wooden stand and table beneath the arrangement, and their pointed stems lead the eye to the swag above.

In the swag the analogy is repeated in different tempo. Orange and red-orange dominate; green and yellow are subordinate. Magnolia leaves, now aged and dried, are reversed to imitate carved wood. Their upper surfaces of gray-green afford contrast in texture and color with green-yellow and red-orange cockscomb. Rosettes of pine cones, cut to simulate flower heads, add a co-ordinating sculptured form. A dried pineapple, symbol of hospitality, crowns the whole and balances the green leaves angled below. (This composition is known irreverently to my friends as "the quick and the dead"!)

Plate 7. *From an Ocean Garden*

The spectrum hues of earth's surface-life are repeated in the vast world under the sea. Here are tiny fish whose eggs are like emeralds scintillating fathoms down; animals of such exquisite color and form that we give them flower names, as sea anemone and sea lily, and shells and sea fans and pearls which exploit the spectrum with every ray of light.

There is an iridescence in all forms of marine life more evident than is visible on land, as if unfamiliar sunlight called forth a special radiance. In the sea depths where sunlight never penetrates, the lamps of divers reveal an amazing phenomenon: colors appear quite opposite, and blood from a wound looks green not red.

In the fish-store window is a display often more chromatic than that of the decorator's nearby. Lobsters of seaweed-green have blue-green markings sparked with pure orange-red. The blue-green claws of crabs enliven the more subtle analogy of green-and-yellow bodies. No wonder the ocean furnishes our color vocabulary with coral, shrimp, shell-pink, amber, aquamarine, ultramarine, salmon, and seal-brown. Fog, mist, oyster-white, and sand suggest more subtle values. These names by association lure us to the color of sea gardens.

Plate 8. *Sea Reflections—a Complementary Harmony*

Nothing in this arrangement is of marine origin yet it reflects the ocean composition. It is the response of the June garden to a challenge tossed up by the sea; a repetition in line and form and color, but with greater elegance of texture. The sweeping branches of the Atlas cedar might be giant seaweed wrenched from coral rock. The shell-like petals of the oriental poppies move in every breeze as if stirred by ocean current. Unobtrusively the tritoma affords a transition of line and form as it simulates spikes of coral.

This is a direct complementary harmony despite incidental, and quite inconsequential, evidence of a third hue. All plants are bold in line and form, and intense in chroma. The weight and bulk of the ancient incense burner demanded their large scale. Chevreul's law of "simultaneous contrast" is obvious in the blue-green and red-orange, each making the other more vibrant than either would appear alone.

While textures are dominantly smooth and fine, and compatible with the container, the evergreen provides stimulating contrast. This is a simple arrangement, depending upon its elements for drama and upon fidelity to principles of design for coordination.

So often a sea shell restricts our thought so that we cannot divorce use from origin. Let shell colors suggest a composition derived from your own perennial border.

Plate 9.   Cardinal Virtues

To me, there is no more resplendent red nor one with a higher saturation of chroma than that of the cardinal flower. This splendid wildflower, Lobelia cardinalis, one of the choicest and rarest, is a radiant example of what the perceptive eye can find in Nature.

The plant shows a direct complementary harmony in which red dominates through sheer impact of chroma, for the green, made stronger by contrast, actually is high in chroma also. Each blossom up and down the stalk is like a high-powered lamp. Fortunately, many of us have been able to grow it by planting seeds in the moist soil it loves. To pick the cardinal flower in the wild is to destroy next year's crop; to plant seeds in your own garden is good conservation.

Coming upon a group of cardinal flowers by a woodland brook, we are often so struck by the intense color of the spires that we fail to notice the perfection of design revealed in each floret. The twins in the picture reveal each detail clearly as they proudly flourish gray and white topknots which crown the red styles. Surely this is a flower with personality, and a colorful one. An intimate study like this proves once again that we must look closely not to miss some of the useful lessons taught by Nature, and that perhaps we should learn more if our hunting equipment included a magnifying glass as well as the clippers we always carry.

Plate 10.   Nature's Dominants Reversed

It was fun to reproduce the cardinal flower's colors in an arrangement with green rather than red as the dominant. This composition started with the impressive sculptured form of an unusual variety of echeveria, with fluted edges outlined in sharp red. The red candle was also a strong structure, less than spectrum intensity in color yet a worthy opponent in visual weight. These two forms established the structural pattern. After several experiments with fruits and flowers, red plums and cherries proved a good choice, varied in scale but similar in hue and value. They were placed to follow the downward spiral of the candle.

The arrangement still lacked emphasis and my search continued for a repetitive form in green. This was difficult for the echeveria was a grayed value of almost spectrum green. I tried limes—too yellow-green; seedless grapes—the same. Peppers and green tomatoes were too coarse and lacked transitional form. Then came the inspiration; unripe Concord grapes would be of proper scale and agreeable hue. They could add support to the echeveria with both form and color. Which color dominates? I believe it is green because of its dramatic form and its prominent placement. Do you agree?

The "hurricane glass" is a globe from a street lamp, generous in scale and proportion for such large-scale units.

Plate 11.   Color from Underground

Precious gems and semiprecious stones hold a colorful lure which few of us can resist. The display of a great ruby or sapphire makes headline news. Seldom can a layman reconcile the beauty of a polished gem with the dingy rock in the rough. Indeed, many commonplace rocks have more original vibrant color than valuable minerals. The Colorado Canyon is a spectrum in stone, changing hues with every hour of sunlight. A stretch of road construction often unearths limestone of jadelike beauty or serpentine of emerald hue. Copper ore in rocks shows a splendid blue-green; zinc is a silver streak in a rose-colored setting.

Before early painters developed their rich pigments, craftsmen were making pictures from colored stones. Mosaics of Indian or Persian or Byzantine origin retain their original chroma today. Earth colors cover a wide range of tonalities.

The little framed "arrangements" are made from flower-hued stones. At the left, chrysacolla, an intense green-blue, shows the presence of copper; the pendant "cat's eyes" below are a limestone formation. The rose-quartz blossom with the amethyst-quartz center has leaves and stem of topaz. Above, azurite seems aptly named; its delphinium-like discs have yellow buds of sulphur and leaves of carnelian. Jewelers appreciating the beauty of minerals make their own designs of gem-flowers.

We borrow mineral names—amethyst, copper, emerald, garnet, jade, sapphire, slate, chalk, coal, gold, silver, and turquoise—to describe our color sensations, and it seems to me reasonable to believe that the living color of a garden is repeated in older formations underground.

Plate 12. The Jewel Tree—Split Complementary Harmony

The arrangement includes many of the mineral colors of the preceding plate. Even the old French iron urn and the marble plinth are of mineral origin. The design is purposely compact, its conical, treelike mass suggesting a Byzantine mosaic.

The harmony is based on a split complement. The key color is yellow, which in zinnias and daisies threads its way through the pattern, co-ordinating with other hues. Yellow appears in differing values and in varying scale. Vertical balance is maintained by the light red-violet gladiolus and astilbe, both moderately high in chroma. Darker coleus foliage of the same hue adds strength near the base.

Blue-violet hydrangeas set up a circular rhythm which concentrates attention near the center of equilibrium. This dispersal of the values allows the blue-violet to become visible. Blues and violets being receding colors have a tendency to lose much of their rich beauty when they are massed; combined with another color of more vibrant chroma, as here with yellow, a reaction is produced which makes each more effective—another example of the working of the law of simultaneous contrast.

All the flowers came from a July garden. They were selected not only for color but for their simulation of jewel tones. There is no dominant form; each blossom is simply another piece added to the mosaic. Seldom can we design a compact mass and not lose the individuality of flowers. To effect rhythmic line we usually need the voids in silhouette to give depth and motion. But this is a design, somewhat artificial in conception, which makes a point of grouping color in the manner of a mosaic.

Plate *13*.   *Flying Colors*

In the late summer garden only drowsy sounds suggest the business of insects. A pollen-covered bee backs out of a trumpet flower with such accuracy that he loses not a grain of golden freight. A green stem suddenly comes to life as the praying mantis completes his devotions. A brown leaf among other withered leaves wings off with jet-propelled speed, and we know that the dead-leaf butterfly is far from lifeless. At rest, many insects are so monochromatic in appearance that they are well camouflaged; in action, they may safely wear their jewels.

It is a joy to study color on the wing where fine harmonies are revealed only by close examination. We see that the cecropia moth is a handsome fellow in his brownish fur, and we may recognize him from his markings. But how often do we see the devices of red-orange and red-violet on those wing-marks? The black swallowtail butterfly wears an elegant velvet cloak on which we can see his split complementary harmony of yellow and orange and violet-blue.

Even in the less appealing larval stages the sphinx moth and monarch butterfly show colors worth reproducing in fine textiles. The dragon fly is a stained-glass window in flight. Most beautiful of all is the luna moth of ethereal texture and color. His wings of both yellow-green and blue-green are outlined in wine-red-violet; his spots and antennae are spun gold. No flower arrangement can capture this loveliness but its perfection is a marvelous inspiration.

Plate 14.   Lunar Attraction—a Direct Complement

Every change of light turned the wings of the luna moth from blue- to yellow-green so that the coloring almost defied interpretation, and the most delicate blossoms appeared too heavy to suggest the soft texture. Everything had to be fine, nothing commonplace.

Collecting materials for the arrangement consumed two days and involved miles of travel. Fortunately I had access to a private collection of containers from which I chose an old blanc de chine vase and incense burner to suggest the blue-white overtones of the moth. The green curves of bells-of-Ireland followed eagerly the wing-sweep, each green calyx a bowl like that held by the Immortal. Each bell held a tiny flower amazingly like the moth itself.

Ismene leaves placed edge-wise filled a void without being too obvious. Red-violet buddleia supplied the right hue but lacked important form. I was becoming discouraged when a miracle occurred: my hardy amaryllis—always unpredictable—chose to open its first delicately-tinted red-violet blooms, a perfect accent. The large green rosette is water lettuce, a miniature specimen of which provided a "moth" to perch on the porcelain bowl. (I believe the Immortal smiled faintly as I balanced it there.) This unusual water-plant has shell-like leaves marked like the moth's wing. To get the rosette, a large colony of goldfish busily laying eggs had to be displaced, but by this time I was ruthless.

Plate 15.   Forest Pygmies

Immense redwoods and steepled firs are the forest giants of the
West. The older eastern mountains have beech and oak and
spruce with their associates presenting monochromatic harmonies
in fine textural variety. These are the larger gifts of the forest.
The pygmy plants are quite as notable in their way, and perhaps
more exquisite in design and coloration.

Low on the forest floor old logs bear opulent growths of fungi
and lichens and mosses. Edges of mountain streams are rich
sources for investigation. In *The Lichen Book*, Guy Nearing
speaks of "lichens adorning rocks and trees lavishly with their
chaste embroideries. . . . The fruiting tips of one cladonia may
flaunt a vermilion purer than the garden's most treasured flower
while goblets of another might serve as models for the acme of
the potter's art." Their infinite subtleties of color and the won-
drous textures of these small plants are fascinating to discover.

The picture includes many kinds of mosses and lichens and
fungi, most of them collected within a limited area and in a short
space of time. An exception is the rarer "old man's beard" lichen
at the top of the group. The emphasis here is on texture rather
than diversity of color. The specimens are posed to suggest a
wooded mountain with rocks and a stream bed winding down.
In the sculptured form of these pygmies we learn to appreciate
muted colors and varied textures. In addition to grayed yellows
and greens, coral, gold, and violet are sometimes found.

Plate 16.   Emphasis on Texture—an Analogous Harmony

There is surprising kinship between the lichens and fungi of the
preceding picture and this sophisticated composition. This is due
to similarity of subtle color values and also to textural qualities.
While the harmony is generally analogous, no effort was made to
restrict the range so yellow and blue are both included. Component parts were selected primarily to focus attention on tex-

tures. While Nature supplied all materials for the first study, craftsmen produced the container and textile used here.

The vase is modern Italian, an unusually fine piece of a cunning large design which tapers to a short slender neck. Its great beauty lies in the way texture has modified intense colors, for the basic glazes are strong yellow and green-blue skillfully blended with a rough gray overlay. The result is deceptively ancient; this might be a long-buried Egyptian vase.

The textile, also modern, is based on a design from an old Chinese bowl. Faithful to the grayed yellows, blues, and greens, the fabric is made more emphatic by the use of black, white, and gray.

Since much of its charm lies in the contour, the neck of the vase has not been obscured. A bare beech branch spirals upward and is continued downward with hydrangeas curving behind and then re-appearing. Small yellow day lilies strike a contrasting note of bright color and smooth texture—yet they stand free of the vase so as not to obscure the outline.

EARLY CONTRIBUTORS TO
THE SCIENCE OF COLOR

Sir Isaac Newton (1642-1727)
>His experiment with light rays disclosed the spectrum band
>which is the basis of color charts. It was Newton who be-
>lieved that the spectrum could be made into a continuous
>band based on a circle.

Christian Huygens (1629-1695)
>Helped to stimulate the theory that light and color travel in
>wave lengths.

George Field (1774-1854)
>Set forth a theory that there can be harmony wherever a
>primary hue is present.

Michel Chevreul (1786-1889)
>Stated the laws of color harmony and contrast.

Ewald Hering (1834-1918)
>Advanced the study of the physiological aspects of color.

Hermann von Helmholtz (1821-1894)
>Developed theories on the relationship of color and optics.

Wilhelm Ostwald (1853-1932)
>Physicist and philosopher whose equation is the basis for
>many modern color systems.

It may surprise the student to learn that Goethe, whom we know
primarily as a great German poet and Schopenhauer as a philosopher,
each did considerable research in color, the latter being the first to
declare that color is "sensation." Their interest is an indication of
the universal lure of the subject in all fields.

FOR FURTHER READING

Principles of Color and Color Mixing by Jacques Bustanoby. McGraw-Hill, N. Y., 1947

Basic Color by Egbert Jacobsen. Paul Theobald, Chicago, 1948

Colors: What They Can Do For You by Louis Cheskin. Liveright Publishing Company, N. Y., 1947

Color Fundamentals by Maitland Graves. McGraw-Hill, N. Y., 1952

A Color Notation by Albert H. Munsell. Munsell Color Company, Inc., Baltimore, 10th Edition, 1946

A Dictionary of Color by A. Maerz and M. R. Paul. McGraw-Hill, N. Y., 1930

*Historical Guide To Color by Elizabeth Burris-Meyer. Helburn, N. Y., 1938

*The Principles of Harmony and Contrast of Colours by Michel E. Chevreul. Bell, London, 1890

*The Language of Color by Matthew Luckiesh. Dodd, N. Y., 1918

*The Enjoyment and Use of Color by Walter Sargent. C. Scribner's Sons, N. Y., 1923

*Color Standards and Color Nomenclature by Robert Ridgeway. Published by the author, Washington, D. C., 1912

* Indicates out-of-print books. These are not in the regular stock of publishers and bookstores. They can sometimes be bought in the second-hand book market. Your local librarian may be able to borrow copies of these books on an inter-library loan or through your state library agency.

Color-aid Swatch Book compiled by Sidney Beller may be obtained from National Council Books Inc., Box 4298, Philadelphia 44

COLOR THEMES FOR
FLOWER-SHOW CLASSES

INDEX